Course Studies – Tracking Ontario's Thames:
An Exploration of the River

George Thomas Kapelos

with Steven Evans, Photographer

Museum London, London, Ontario, 2001

Table of Contents

From the Sponsor

IT IS INDEED A PLEASURE for Trojan Technologies Inc. to assist in the sponsorship of *Course Studies - Tracking Ontario's Thames: An Exploration of the River* exhibition and publication. By making this gesture we are restating our commitment to Museum London and to the arts community of our fair city.

Allan Bulckaert, President and CEO
Trojan Technologies Inc.

Foreword

MUSEUM LONDON IS PROUD to be presenting the exhibition *Course Studies - Tracking Ontario's Thames: An Exploration of the River*. For those of us living in London, Ontario, and indeed for all of those who live along the Thames, the river is a part of our daily life. We pass over it on our way to work, walk along it for recreation and solace, and recognize it as an important factor in the life and history of the region.

Capturing and communicating the complex subject of the river has been the task of the *Course Studies* exhibition team. Guest curator George Thomas Kapelos is to be commended for the insights he has brought to the subject, Lynne DiStefano has ably set out the historical context of ninteenth century settlement along the river, and Steven Evans' compelling photographs convey the diversity one finds along the river.

Exhibitions like *Course Studies - Tracking Ontario's Thames: An Exploration of the River* do not occur without the generosity and foresight of others. I would like to sincerely thank the Richard Ivey Foundation, the Museums Assistance Program of the Canadian Heritage Department, Trojan Technologies Inc., and the Ontario Arts Council for their support of this project. Sponsoring this exhibition, and even more importantly for its long-lasting contribution, this publication, is recognition of the value and importance of cultural and historical scholarship as it relates to London and region.

Museum London staff have also made a significant contribution to *Course Studies - Tracking Ontario's Thames: An Exploration of the River*. Our Curator of Regional History Mike Baker has assisted the exhibition team throughout the entire process and Bob Ballantine has once again designed a handsome catalogue to showcase the work of the writers and photographer.

Course Studies - Tracking Ontario's Thames: An Exploration of the River is an exhibition that reflects our area's rich culture and heritage, and forms an important contribution to the understanding of our collective past and present.

Brian Meehan, Executive Director
Museum London

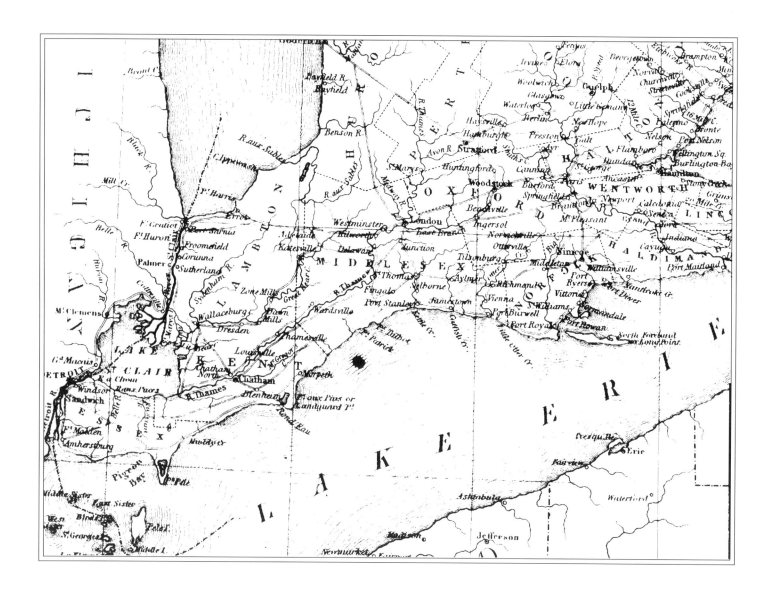

The river Thames lies like an uncoiled lash across the face of Southwestern Ontario. Its muddied waters, unhurried except in flood, are garnered from many streams drawing tribute from the peninsula.

— Fred Coyne Hamil, *The Valley of the Lower Thames: 1640 to 1850*

Introduction

by George Thomas Kapelos

SPREAD OUT A MAP and it is easy to locate the Thames: two branches uniting in one place, forming a river that meanders across the rich Ontario hinterland, before it quietly empties into Lake St. Clair, part of Canada's Great Lakes waterways system. (See fig. 1.) Look closer: the two branches and main channel are themselves branching systems, supported by smaller streams, creeks, drainage ditches and rivulets. Along the channel, the river widens where artificial lakes have been made. Contour maps show smaller channels, cut through the glacial uplands, bringing spring runoffs to the river and its tributaries. Cartography only begins to tell the river's story. While the river exists plainly as a part of Ontario's geography, it also exists as a perception that can be dissected and understood.

According to the *Oxford Dictionary,* a river is a "natural flow of water travelling along a channel to the sea, a lake or another river." This is certainly the Thames. A second definition suggests other meanings: "a large quantity of a flowing substance." But what might these other substances be? Materials carried by the water? Can other materials, aside from water, flow in a river? Indeed, the flow of a river can be understood to contain more abstract notions such as time, human emotion, and ideas.

Growing up in London, I have always been aware of the river. That awareness was peripheral and incidental, consisting of early memories of the river intertwined with my own history. Picnics at Springbank Park and bucolic excursions along the river's edge left me with the imprint of the Thames as a pastoral refuge. But the Thames is also associated with my first encounter with death. I still shudder when I think of a sailboat trip on Fanshawe Lake that turned terrifying. Our boat was almost capsized during a sudden summer thunderstorm; it took all the skill of a friend to bring us safely back to shore. A visit to a local London restaurant was not complete without my mother's pointing out a line on the dining room wall showing the high water mark of the 1937 flood. This was a

Fig. 1. Southwestern Ontario in the 1850s.

Detail, map of Canada West, formerly Upper Canada, published by Thomas Cowperthwait, Philadelphia 1850.

reminder of the river's power, when a spring surge inundated a large part of the city. I am certain my own personal imprint of the Thames is repeated with variation among those Londoners who have come in contact with it.

But the river extends beyond London. From springs, freshets, marshes and depressions in the farm fields around Mitchell, Embro or Tavistock in the east, the slow meandering course works its way by the nations of the Munsee Delaware, Oneida of the Thames, Chippewa of the Thames, and Delaware of Moraviantown, politely bisecting Chatham, hemmed in by dykes, and passing large prosperous farms of more recent Canadians in Lambton and Kent, before arriving at its mouth. The river is place, memory, destination and definer to over half a million people. Multiply the meaning of the river by these inhabitants and the stories of this place become infinite. And each story is different.

Beyond that is the question of what we understand by the Thames. Is it merely the river that commands our attention, or is it more? Certainly the river has been the central artery and the vehicle for exploration of a territory, as Lynne DiStefano's essay points out. For these early visitors, as well as for all past and present inhabitants, the river is inseparable from the landscape that contains it. As system, place and idea, river and landscape are linked.

Defining and interpreting *landscape* are central preoccupations of those interested in the analysis of contemporary environments. Scholars from a wide variety of disciplines, including geography, cultural studies, design and ecology, embrace this field of study. At its centre is the late John Brinkerhoff Jackson (1909 – 1996). Noted for his observations on the North American landscape, Jackson asks, "Why is it … that we have trouble agreeing on the meaning of *landscape*? The word is simple enough, and it refers to something which we think we understand; and yet to each of us it seems to mean something different."[1] Beginning with this simple question, Jackson proceeds to unpack the word, giving us a sense that *landscape* cannot be a single, common idea, but is a concept of complexity and multiplicity. The study of the watercourse therefore cannot be just one study, but rather it becomes a series, aptly, of *concurrent* explorations. Just as the Thames is made up of branches and tributaries, each distinct but contributing to the system as a whole, so is the reading of this river's landscape.

For Jackson, elements that give shape to the concept of *landscape* include spaces on the earth's surface and human interventions. "A landscape is where we speed up or retard or divert the cosmic program and impose our own."[2] Thus, landscape is linked to human occupation and use, to cultural conditions and attitudes. Further, and

1. J. B. Jackson, *Discovering the Vernacular Landscape,* p. 1.
2. J. B. Jackson, *Discovering the Vernacular Landscape,* p. 156.

more significantly, landscape is linked to time, or, as Marcea Eliade points out, "it represents man taking upon himself the role of time."[3] For Jackson, landscape and culture are indistinguishable. "No group sets out to create a landscape … what it sets out to do is create a community, and the landscape as its visible manifestation is simply the by-product of people working and living."[4]

The studies that follow contribute to an understanding of Ontario's Thames River as a totality. However, each contributor speaks from a singular point of view, bringing his or her own experiences to this exploration. Historian and conservationist Lynne DiStefano draws from early travellers' accounts. As an architect and urbanist, I have chosen to explore the ways in which the river's environment has been constructed. Photographer Steven Evans captures specific views of the river at a contemporary moment in time.

For each of us, the Thames is not a static entity but one of change, dynamism and flow. To clarify this narration, the following metaphorical expressions, or *tropes,* have been chosen to identify our work: *Voice, Order, System, Time* all creating *Place*, and *Picture*. But each of these *tropes* has in itself a flowing definition. *Voice* records the shift in the tone of narratives from exploration and discovery to adventure and reflection. *The Constructed Landscape* is presented as an equation: *(order + system + time)/vernacular = place*. Within this equation, *Order* begins as an idea in the wilderness and progresses to an ordering of nature. *System* starts as navigation and orientation and moves to ecology and flow. *Time* is also a shifting entity. Early accounts of the river reveal its history, while later accounts seek both to preserve and recreate this history. For other narrators, the river's time is greater than its written history. Together this equation, when experienced through the lens of the local condition or the *vernacular,* creates *Place*, an experience that remains with the beholder beyond the immediate moment. Finally, *Picture,* Steven Evans' black and white photographs shot in the past year, become another account of the river, taken by one photographer and presented for the interpretation of the viewer.

Through our experience of a landscape, be it by means of historical accounts, by interpreting specific human constructions, or by taking and looking at photographs, the Thames landscape has the capacity to create sustained mental images and sensations of vividness and detail, even when we are apart from it. As James Corner defines it, this is landscape's *eidetic* potential.[5] Unequivocally, the Thames exists as a landscape of beauty, history and power. Taken together this is a landscape we profoundly appreciate. The multiple understandings of the Thames River give us a strong sense of what is called *Place*. And this sense of *Place* is simultaneously universal and highly personal.

3. Marcea Eliade, "La Terre-mère et les Hierogamies cosmiques," *Eranos Jahrbuch* (1953) as cited in J. B. Jackson, *Discovering the Vernacular Landscape*, p. 8.
4. J. B. Jackson, *Discovering the Vernacular Landscape*, p. 12.
5. James Corner, *Recovering Landscape*, p. 153.

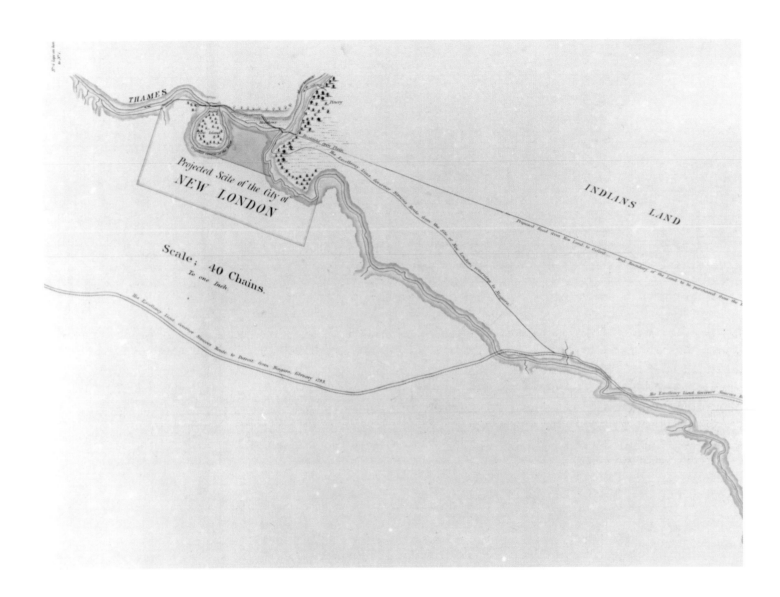

THAMES

Projected Scite of the City of
NEW LONDON

Scale; 40 Chains.
To one Inch.

INDIAN'S LAND

Voice:
British and Canadian Travel Narratives, 1793-1891

by Lynne DiStefano

Travels along the Thames occurred for a variety of reasons. In the late eighteenth and early nineteenth centuries, people — the British in particular — were eager to explore and promote Upper Canada. By the mid-nineteenth century, travellers along the Thames had less interest in exploring but more in documenting the state of settlement. Toward the latter part of the century, travellers were preoccupied with the pursuit of pleasure through tourist-related activities, in what can loosely be called adventure tourism. Essentially, early travels revealed a river relatively untouched by Europeans, while later travels occurred in a landscape largely shaped by European settlement. The subtler shaping of the landscape by Aboriginal peoples was largely ignored by these earlier travellers and for the most part was invisible to them.

Fig. 2. Detail, *Survey of the River La Tranche or Thames*, c. 1795.

National Map Collection, Public Archives of Canada

In 1793, in his search for a site for the future capital of Upper Canada, Lieutenant Governor Simcoe discovered a "capital situation eminently calculated for the metropolis of all Canada" at the forks of La Tranche (the Thames) (Littlehales, p. 12). In this detail of the *Survey of the River La Tranche or Thames* (c. 1795), Simcoe's route is marked in red in the original (and appears as a dark line in the reproduction). The future site of London is clearly indicated and labelled as: "Projected Scite of the City of NEW LONDON."

Fig. 3. George Russell Dartnell, *St. Marys on the Thames, 1842.*
watercolour over graphite on paper, with scraping

Private Collection. Photo: Royal Ontario Museum

A very early watercolour of the Thames at St. Marys, executed by George Russell Dartnell, a recognized artist and a member of the Becher hunting expedition of 1842. The primitive state of settlement is apparent, and the river flats are obscured by dense forest. The piers for the first St. Marys bridge are shown, and two of the town's earliest buildings — a stone gristmill and small log house — are also included (Pfaff, p. 94).

Exploration

This narration begins in 1793 with the memorable winter journey of Lieutenant Governor Simcoe and his small party, who, travelling from Niagara by foot, sleigh, cariole and horseback, sought a site for the future capital of Upper Canada. [1]

The Thames figures prominently in the journal kept by one of the party's members, Major Littlehales, "a well-bred, mild and amiable man."[2] On the outward journey, Littlehales tersely records the group's first encounter with the Thames, on February 12:

> We passed a few cedar Groves, and about 1 o'clock crossed on the trunk of a tree a small branch of La Tranche (Thames) and soon afterwards crossed the main branch of that river in the same manner.[3]

1. Edward Baker Littlehales, "Journal from Niagara to Detroit," 1, pp. 288-93.
2. Major Littlehales is so described by the French Duke de Liancourt (presumably Duc de La Rochefoucauld-Liancourt). His comments are quoted by Henry Scadding in his introduction to Littlehales' *Journal.* See Edward Baker Littlehales, *Journal,* p. 3.
3. Littlehales, p. 289.

After this encounter, La Tranche, as the river was then called, is cited repeatedly in the major's journal, frequently as an obstacle to cross, but more usually as a potential transportation route. On March 2, as the party is heading homewards, it stops for an entire day at "the forks of the river," the future site of London.[4] (See fig. 2.) As Littlehales writes, this site "possesses the following advantages: Command of Territory — internal situation — central position — facility of water communication up and down the Thames — superior navigation for boats to near its source, and for small crafts, probably to the Moravian settlement…"[5]

Littlehales' account describes fauna, flora and Aboriginal settlements along the river. However, there is little room for pleasure or adventure. Simcoe and his party are on a mission of discovery. For them, the Thames is a resource waiting to be exploited.

In a similar spirit, a young Charles Aikins rides out from Sandwich (Windsor) in the summer of 1806 to visit his uncle in York (Toronto). His *Journal of a Journey* notes, on June 28: "arrived at River Thames at sunset, and had some difficulty to get my horse over the bridge, at the first fork [Baptiste Creek] of the Thames, as it was very miry on each side."[6] Later he writes, with understandable feelings of accomplishment (or perhaps exasperation): "In coming from Boyez' to Allen's [Delaware] *I forded the River Thames four times.*"[7]

In Aikins' account, the river is barely described. Rather he is more interested in statistics — distances travelled and the number of mills en route. Clearly biased toward the land, Aikins concludes: "I am quite happy that I came by that road, for I am now much better acquainted with the country than I could be from information."[8]

Promotion

Aikins' preoccupation with quantifying the landscape anticipates Robert Gourlay's impressive *Statistical Account of Upper Canada,* published in 1822. For his survey, Gourlay sent out a 31-point questionnaire in 1817 to each township in Upper Canada. The next-to-last question straightforwardly asks, "if [there is the presence of] any water conveyance."[9] Township after township within the Thames watershed responded with detailed information. From Raleigh, at the lower reaches of the river, came this observation:

The Thames, which washes the north west bank of this township, affords those near it an excellent

4. Littlehales, p. 293.
5. Littlehales, p. 293.
6. Charles Aikins, "Journal of a Journey," p.15.
7. Charles Aikins, "Journal of a Journey," p.16.
8. Charles Aikins, "Journal of a Journey," p.19.
9. Robert Gourlay, *Statistical account of Upper Canada,* 1, p. 274.

means of conveyance, there being from 18 to 20 feet water in the river, and from six to seven feet on the bar where it empties into Lake St. Clair, which affords water enough for small vessels to enter or go out loaded.[10]

And from Oxford, near the upper reaches:

The navigation of the river is capable of improvement, by removing some obstructions, and deepening the channel in some places.[11]

Gourlay's main purpose was to encourage emigration. Adequate conveyance by water or road was critical to settlement and, for many townships, the Thames was an important communication link.

In 1821, one year before Gourlay's account appeared, John Howison's *Sketches of Upper Canada* was published. Although this work includes "Practical Details for the Information of Emigrants of Every Class," Howison's main text is a series of descriptions couched as "letters." "Letter XII" includes observations on the Thames, made in early winter in the midst of a "drifting snow-storm."[12] In spite of this, Howison's appreciation of the river is clear:

The course of the Thames is beautiful and meandering; its waters are delightfully transparent; and it can be navigated by large vessels thirty miles above its mouth.[13]

Howison's interest in practical matters relating to immigration compels him to comment on the river's bounty and the quality of its adjacent lands. However, he is less generous in his description of the settlers on both sides of the river and baldly declares, "Canadians … are very bad farmers."[14]

Pleasure and Reflection

Howison's account represents an important shift in the way the Thames is perceived. More than a "facility of water communication" or a "conveyance," the river is increasingly viewed as a thing of beauty.

Anna Brownell Jameson's *Winter Studies and Summer Rambles in Canada*, published in 1838, recounts her travels

10. Robert Gourlay, *Statistical account of Upper Canada*, 1, pp. 288-89.
11. Robert Gourlay, *Statistical account of Upper Canada*, 1, p. 309.
12. John Howison, *Sketches of Upper Canada*, p. 199.
13. John Howison, *Sketches of Upper Canada*, p. 207.
14. John Howison, *Sketches of Upper Canada*, pp. 207-8.

by cart from Woodstock to Chatham. Jameson repeatedly refers to the river as "beautiful."[15] Near Woodstock, it is "a small but most beautiful stream, winding like the Isis at Oxford."[16]

Jameson, however, does not see perfection in everything. As she writes during her Chatham visit:

> As I travel on, I am disgusted, or I am enchanted; I despair or I exult by turns; and these inconsistent and apparently contradictory emotions and impressions I set down as they arise, leaving you to reconcile them as well as you can…[17]

While Jameson was appraising the visual qualities of the Thames, other writers assessed the river for its impact on settlement. Predating Jameson by eight years, Joseph Pickering in his *Emigration or No Emigration* glowingly described the Thames as "a fine stream," whose flats "are the richest land in the province; the soil in some parts a loamy fat clay, covered by a rich black mould … in other places a sandy or gravelly loam, dry, rich, and well watered with springs." [18]

"Well-watered" is a familiar expression in emigrant guides of the 1830s. In *The British Dominions*, written by Joseph Bouchette and published in 1832, the Thames flows through districts described as "well watered."[19] Similar terminology is used in 1833 in *The Canadas*. Here descriptions vary between "watered by the river Thames" to "partly watered by the Thames" to "well watered throughout"[20] — not very inventive, but pertinent to the task of promoting the region to emigrants.

Adventure

The potential of the river to offer adventure is first found in Edward Allen Talbot's account of his *Five Years' Residence in the Canadas* (1824). In the context of describing fish found in Canada's rivers and lakes, Talbot embarks on a fish tale of amazing proportions:

> Sturgeons of an immense size are caught in great numbers, in many of the large rivers, and particularly in the Thames. Fishes of this description frequently weigh 150 lbs., and measure seven feet in length. In the Spring of the year, they, like every other fish in America except the Salmon, come up the rivers from the large lakes, to deposit their spawn.[21]

15. Anna Brownell Jameson, *Winter Studies and Summer Rambles in Canada*, pp. 241-312.
16. Anna Brownell Jameson, *Winter Studies and Summer Rambles in Canada*, p. 242.
17. Anna Brownell Jameson, *Winter Studies and Summer Rambles in Canada*, p. 303.
18. Joseph Pickering, *Emigration or no emigration*, pp. 60-61.
19. Joseph Bouchette, *The British Dominions in North America*,1, p. 93.
20. [Francis Fairplay], *The Canadas as they now are*, Pt. 2, pp. 93-94, 96.
21. Edward Allen Talbot, *Five years' residence in the Canadas*,1, p. 268.

This straightforward narrative soon becomes farfetched:

> In the Spring of 1821, an intimate acquaintance of mine … was one day fishing on the Canadian Thames, accompanied by his son … Observing an uncommonly large Sturgeon sailing up the river, the son immediately pierced it with his spear, and, retaining a firm hold of his weapon, was dragged into the water. For some time he floated on the stream, behind the Sturgeon, by the aid of his instrument; but, at length becoming weary of this disagreeable mode of proceeding, like another Aristus, he got astride of the fish, and converting his spear into a bridle-rein, rode him for nearly a mile down the river…[22]

In the end, the fish dies from loss of blood, but Talbot awards the poor creature a hero's epitaph: "[he] yielded up his life to the prowess of his rider."[23]

The thirst for adventure, especially in the guise of hunting, is vividly described in two mid-nineteenth-century accounts. The first, a "shooting excursion," in October 1842, involves a hunting trip from London to the "Falls in the River Thames" at St. Marys.[24] The excursion party, made up of four notable Londoners, included George Russell Dartnell, a British army surgeon and watercolorist, and Henry C.R. Becher, a London lawyer.[25] Becher considered the excursion so memorable that he wrote a lively account entitled "The Pirate of St. Mary's," published in the 7 January 1843 edition of New York's *Albion*.[26] The pirate is none other than the "tall Yankee chopper" (woodsman) who built the party's boat for their adventure down the Thames.[27]

Becher quipped that the party had so many "eatables and drinkables … [and] buffalo skins" that it looked like "a trip to the Rocky Mountains," rather than one to St. Marys. Nevertheless, after a day and a half of travel on bad roads, the group managed to reach its rather disappointing destination.[28] (See fig. 3.) They had expected to find "a fine flourishing little place, with a wild roaring cataract beside it." When the party enquired about the location of "the Falls," they were shown "the rapid by the mill, with a fall at the head of it of about two feet. And this, and two or three other rapids with similar sharp tumbles at their beginning, were the *Falls* [they] had come so far to see."[29]

22. Edward Allen Talbot, *Five years' residence in the Canadas,*1, p. 269.
23. Edward Allen Talbot, *Five years' residence in the Canadas,*1, p. 269.
24. I am grateful to Larry Pfaff for information about the St. Marys' "shooting excursion." See H[enry] [C.R.] B[echer], "The Pirate of St. Mary's," *New York Albion*, 7 January 1843, pp. 4-5. The reference to the "Falls" appears on p. 4.
25. Larry Pfaff, *Historic St. Marys*, p. 94.
26. The article is dated "London, Canada West, Oct., 1842."
27. [C.R.] B[echer], "The Pirate of St. Mary's," pp. 4-5.
28. [C.R.] B[echer], "The Pirate of St. Mary's," p. 4.
29. [C.R.] B[echer], "The Pirate of St. Mary's," p. 4.

Only on the third day did the river adventure properly start. In order to avoid the bad roads on their return to London, the party was promised a custom-made boat by the "chopper" the day before.[30] Becher writes that "We were all up at daylight . . . to see the boat, which was just being launched. It was built of green basswood boards just from the mill, and looked very much like an overgrown lumber waggon [sic] box."[31] Once properly caulked, the boat was declared seaworthy and the party, having stowed its possessions, "embarked, and with three mock cheers from the boat-builders, bade adieu to St. Mary's.[32] The description of the trip is worth recounting for it was, in every sense of the word, an adventure:

> After coming down a rapid, and shipping a good deal of water, which gained on us at a fearful pace, we were in great danger of sinking in a deep spot of the river; the water was half way up to our knees in the boat, but we managed to get in shoal water in time, and were soon all right ...[33]

Eventually, the "worst" rapids finished, the party found the voyage "delightful," and by evening they reached the ford some 20 miles below St. Marys where their wagon was waiting for them.[34]

The second mid-nineteenth-century account, *L'Acadie* (1849), relates several adventures on the Thames, including a rehash of the dramatic fish tale of Edward Allen Talbot. Conceived as a series of explorations in British America, the book was written by Sir James E. Alexander, a colonel of considerable wit, who at one point had been stationed in London with the garrison. His spirit of adventure is best illustrated by his account of a "water hunt" on the Thames — or, to quote Alexander — our "manner of killing deer in the dog days."[35]

Water hunts occurred at night. For Alexander's Thames adventure, two canoes were filled with rushes, to provide comfortable seating for the hunting party, and the first canoe, lit up with a "jack-light," assumed the lead, while the other canoe followed at some distance.[36] As Alexander relates:

> The night was quite calm, which was favourable for the jack-light. It appeared like a bright star on the water, whilst the board behind it threw the canoe and the hunters completely into shade. The deer, as they stand up to their knees in the water ... lift their heads from grazing on the aquatic grass, and gaze with curiosity on the light till it is quite close to them, that is, within twelve or twenty yards, when the crack of the rifle at once ends their fatal curiosity.[37]

30. [C.R.] B[echer], "The Pirate of St. Mary's," p. 4.
31. [C.R.] B[echer], "The Pirate of St. Mary's," p. 5.
32. [C.R.] B[echer], "The Pirate of St. Mary's," p. 5.
33. [C.R.] B[echer], "The Pirate of St. Mary's," p. 5.
34. [C.R.] B[echer], "The Pirate of St. Mary's," p. 5.
35. James Edward Alexander, *L'Acadie*, 1, p. 266.
36. James Edward Alexander, *L'Acadie*, 1, p. 264.
37. James Edward Alexander, *L'Acadie*, 1, p. 264.

Fig. 4. James Hamilton, *Great Western Railroad Cove Bridge, London (Ontario)*, 1874.
pen and ink, with watercolour, on paper

Toronto Reference Library (T.P.L.) J. Ross Robertson Collection, T 15403.

The advent of rail travel significantly changed transportation patterns along the Thames. In this view of London's Cove Bridge the focus is on the passage of a Great Western train. The Thames is a bucolic backdrop complete with grazing cows, and a geographic feature to be "conquered" by nineteenth-century bridge building.

While adventurers in the 1840s found excitement on the Thames, other writers continued to see the river primarily as a source of quiet appreciation, particularly in the framework of the picturesque. In *Eight Years in Canada* (1847), Major Richardson reflects that "no part of the Canadian scenery is more lovely than what is presented, on leaving Chatham, by the windings of the narrow and picturesque Thames."[38] In 1849, the same year as Alexander's account of the "water hunt" appeared, a new edition of Sir Richard Henry Bonnycastle's *Canada and the Canadians* was also published. In his travels by horse and wagon along the Thames, Bonnycastle's descriptions of the river and its landscape are laden with the adjective "beautiful,"[39] and one of the scenes, near Thamesville, is described as "very fine and picturesque." [40]

Interlude: Recitation and Description

During the 1850s and 1860s there is a decided change in the tone of travellers' accounts. The first-person effusiveness of earlier narratives is replaced by rather dry recitations of facts and descriptions of places. In accounts such as William Chambers' *Things As They Are* (1854), the anonymous *The Canadian Tourist* (1856), Charles Mackay's *Life and Liberty in America* (1859), John Disturnell's *The Great Lakes, or Inland Seas of America*

38. John Richardson, *Eight years in Canada*, p. 132.
39. Richard Henry Bonnycastle, *Canada and the Canadians*, 2, pp. 97-105.
40. Richard Henry Bonnycastle, *Canada and the Canadians*, 2, p. 106.

(1863), and Alexander Monro's *History, Geography, and Statistics of British North America* (1864), the Thames is frequently dismissed as a destination without interest.

William Chambers, for example, extols the construction of railways at the expense of natural waterways such as the Thames.[41] In *The Canadian Tourist*, the Thames is merely a geographical reference point for the city of London — "beautifully situated on the River Thames" — and, as in Chambers' account, railway communication is seen as a decided advantage.[42] (See fig. 4.)

Charles Mackay barely saw the Thames — his tour extended to the western part of the province only as far as London. He probably should have eliminated London and the Thames altogether, as, among other things, he had limited enthusiasm for Simcoe's choice of names for the settlement and its river:

> The name of the place and river was originally "The Forks"; but when its early founder absurdly chose to call it London, the river, on the high bank of which it is built, was with equal absurdity miscalled the Thames.[43]

John Disturnell's guide, intended for the "pleasure traveller and emigrant," is a compact compendium of useful information.[44] The Thames is seen as a tributary of the Great Lakes, and, although considered one of "the principal Rivers that are navigable for any considerable length," its actual navigable length is cited as only 24 miles.[45] This relegation of the river to a navigational statistic is in sharp contrast to the guide's descriptive account of the "Railroad Route from Niagara Falls to Hamilton and Detroit, *via* Great Western Railway of Canada."[46] The description of the route includes several references to the Thames, but other than a clear acknowledgement of its navigational importance below Chatham, the river receives little attention.

Tourism

The tendency to ignore the Thames in mid-nineteenth-century accounts such as those mentioned above probably reflects the diminishing importance of the river as a communication link. However, for a small group of travellers, the river retained its attractiveness, but for very different reasons — the opportunity to hunt and fish in earnest, or the opportunity to explore leisurely its natural and cultural heritage. This group of travellers, in fact,

41. William Chambers, *Things as they are in America*, pp. 126-27.
42. Anonymous, *The Canadian Tourist*, p. 17. Elizabeth Waterson, in *the Travellers – Canada to 1900* (Guelph: University of Guelph, 1989), p. 101 describes *The Canadian Tourist* as "a guide book, very widely distributed, solidifying the image of Canadian centres linked by a railway network."
43. Charles Mackay, *Life and liberty in America*, p. 382.
44. John Disturnell, *The Great Lakes or inland seas of North America*.
45. John Disturnell, *The Great Lakes or inland seas of North America*, pp. 15-16.
46. John Disturnell, *The Great Lakes or inland seas of North America*, p. 50.

could well be described as early tourists, with some being decidedly more adventuresome than others. In 1866, H.B. Small's *The Canadian Handbook and Tourist's Guide…with the Best Spots for Fishing and Shooting* singled out the area around the mouth of the Thames for duck shooting:

> The St. Clair flats afford … the finest duck-shooting ground in the world; there, also, may be found the trumpeter swan, the teal, the mallard, the canvass-back, the wood-duck, curlew, snipe, plover, and the birds of prey that invariably hover round these delicious morsels. [47]

Fifteen years later, in 1881, W.E. Saunders and two of his friends rowed down the Thames from London to Lake St. Clair on a shooting expedition. Saunders was only 16 at the time, but his naturalist bent (he would later become a well-known naturalist from London) was already evident in the diary he kept of the trip.[48] The three young men, later described as "the cook" (someone called Hub), "the invalid" (probably Stanley Williams), and "the taxidermist" (probably Saunders), were a memorable crew.[49] "The cook" prepared the daily catch; "the invalid" alternated between helping and complaining, eventually leaving Saunders and Hub to fend for themselves; and "the taxidermist" aggressively hunted his way down the Thames.

On August 18, the first day of the trip, Saunders writes:

> About 5 p.m. today three young Hooded Mergansers flew past us at which we all fired & ingloriously missed. A little further on, however I took revenge on one that tried to rise from the water in front of us. This, with some few Doves and a dozen or so Red-wings formed all our game today.[50]

On day two, after passing the Mooretown Bridge (at Muncey), the young men stopped for a swim. It was here that Saunders notes that:

> there were a number of Leather turtles, Amyda mutica, that were continually poking their heads up & I was tempted to try a shot but of course it had no effect, indeed I doubt that the old fellow stayed on top long enough to get hit. This morning I shot a Red-tailed Hawk & shortly afterwards we passed through the Oneida & Chippewa reserve & saw several squaws washing clothes in the river.[51] (See fig. 5.)

47. Henry Beaumont Small, *The Canadian handbook and tourist's guide*, p. 155.
48. William Edwin Saunders, *Diaries of a Trip to Manitoulin Island*.
49. William Edwin Saunders, *Diaries of a Trip to Manitoulin Island*, p. 29.
50. William Edwin Saunders, *Diaries of a Trip to Manitoulin Island*, p. 21.
51. William Edwin Saunders, *Diaries of a Trip to Manitoulin Island*, p. 21. According to Judd's notes, p. 30, Saunders is mistaken in his identification of the turtle. The species in Ontario is *Trionyx spinifer spinifer* (Eastern Spiny Soft-shelled Turtle), not *Amyda mutica* or, as it is known today, *Trionyx muticus* (Smooth Soft-shelled Turtle).

Fig. 5. William Lees Judson, *The Wishing Well* c.1880.
oil on canvas

Museum London

In Judson's oil, a sweeping curve in the Thames immediately draws the armchair adventurer into the riverscape. The contrast between the gentle river flats on the left bank and the steep and somewhat menacing slopes on the right bank remind the viewer of the changefulness of the river experience. The tepee suggests the multi-layered human history of the Thames watershed — and the rather romantic attraction many travellers felt toward Aboriginals.

On the seventh and last day of the trip, August 24, as the young men, minus "the invalid," are returning to London, Saunders describes the last shoot of the adventure:

> During my swim [near the mouth of the Thames] I saw two large birds flying towards the trees under which Hub was working & I yelled to him that a big hawk was coming right over him; he grabbed his gun & ran out. Just as he came out I said it was an eagle, but when he fired & it dropped, I said, "It's only an old crow after all." In the long grass we couldn't find it but a few minutes afterwards I took another look & our "old crow" proved to be a Raven.[52]

The young hunters were not immune to the beauty of the river. At one point, Saunders observes:

> The most noticeable feature of today was the extreme beauty of some parts of the course. In one place

52. William Edwin Saunders, *Diaries of a Trip to Manitoulin Island*, p. 24.

Fig. 6. William Lees Judson, *The Mouth of the Thames* and *Sea Sick* from *Kühleborn: A Tour of the Thames*, 1881.
lithograph

Museum London

Throughout "Professor Blot's" tour of the Thames, so vividly recorded in prose and image in *Kühleborn: A Tour of the Thames*, are compelling sketches and caricatures of scenes and people along the Thames. Professor Blot (William Lees Judson) not only recorded settlements and riverscapes from London to the mouth of the Thames, but he also provided refreshing vignettes of river people and their activities, including his own.

we could look 300 or 400 yards and all along the river (about 20 yards wide) was a row of willows on each side surmounted by some climber which was just a mass of white bloom all along on top of the willows.[53]

Both the beauty of the river and the challenges of travelling its length and breadth induced "Professor Blot" and his sole companion, young "Frank Lightred," to undertake "a veritable voyage of discovery, with hazy possibilities of difficulties and hardships to be encountered and overcome" in Blot's boat — "a very light double ender, with rudder, oars and lug sail."[54] Their voyage from London to the mouth of the Thames, published in 1881 as *Kühleborn: A Tour of the Thames*, was probably made the summer before. "Professor Blot," the author, was none

53. William Edwin Saunders, *Diaries of a Trip to Manitoulin Island*, p. 22.
54. William Lees Judson, *Kühleborn*, pp. 5-6.

other than William Lees Judson, Paul Peel's teacher and very much an artist in his own right. "Frank Lightred" appears to have been both a "young friend" and fellow artist, and might very well have been Paul Peel.[55] The trip is documented in both prose and sketches.

Although ostensibly described as a tour, the trip should also be seen as a sketching excursion — and a tale of romance. Intermittently, Professor Blot describes sketching locations and laments leaving some of the best spots. He ruminates on the relationship of humans and nature, and repeatedly casts his eye on painterly scenes along the Thames. Near the beginning of the trip, Professor Blot writes:

> Hungerford Hill loomed up as we approached, with its grand possibilities of sylvan and rustic beauty. A pretty pumping house at its base, with a background of dark foliage, floated serenely on its own dimpling reflection.[56]

Before Munceytown, after a picnic on the banks, Professor Blot rests on the grass and reflects — in a most painterly way — on the scene before him:

> Looking down the stream I could see it winding in and out between the promontories until it lost itself in a glint of the shallows under a tall cliff, blue with distance. Nearer, little breezes chased each other over its surface, dimming the reflections with lines and splashes of dusky grey, or flying off to join the cloud shadows on the hillside, when the inverted trees and sky again began to glow through the grey until the water was a perfect mirror again; and again, the rude breeze would rush down upon it like a wanton boy and tear the picture to pieces.[57]

By the time the pair reach the mouth of the Thames, the river is captured in words and drawings. (See fig. 6.) At this point, as well, the romantic subplot in the story reaches a finale, when sweet Miss Annie Lawrie, a member of another party travelling down the Thames at the same time, accepts Frank Lightred's marriage proposal. The tale of the romance seems obviously contrived, but it provides an entertaining counterpoint to the descriptions of the river.

55. William Lees Judson, *Kühleborn*, p. 5. Nancy Poole "strongly suspects, based on her research and contemporary sources, that the art student was, in fact, Paul Peel." Nancy Poole, interview by Edward Phelps, telephone call, London, Ontario, 15 August 2001. Paddy Gunn O'Brien kindly brought the following quote to my attention: "Messrs. W.L. Judson and Paul Peel of this city have just returned from a week's tour down the Thames whither they went for the purpose of sketching." See "Last Minute Locals / A Sketching Tour," *London Advertiser*, 23 July 1877, p. 4.
56. William Lees Judson, *Kühleborn*, p. 6.
57. William Lees Judson, *Kühleborn*, pp. 53-54.

Fig. 7. Arthur J. Stringer, *A Series of Sketches* from "A Confabulatory Canoe Trip," *Chips* (March, 1891).

J.J. Talman Regional Collection, The D.B. Weldon Library, The University of Western Ontario, London, Ontario

The four rather amateur sketches of Stringer and Artemus Warlock's Thames adventure are thumb-scale images of the boys' "thrilling adventures" on the Thames (Stringer, p.25). The trip starts out from London as a rather civilized outing, complete with an umbrella protecting the paddler in the stern (upper left), and the boys' first encampment, initially, seems remarkably straightforward (upper right). On the second day, however, they encounter a "whale" of fish that tests Stringer's mettle (lower left). Near Thamesville the trip becomes a dangerous adventure when a snag in the river capsizes the canoe (lower right).

With *Kühleborn: A Tour of the Thames*, the river is clearly established as a recreational resource "eminently" suited for civilized adventure and romance. And the railway, in replacing the Thames as a transportation means, made pleasure travelling on the river that much easier. Professor Blot was able to return to London with his boat — the *Thirteen* — by rail.[58]

Last Adventure

Some ten years later, Arthur Stringer and one of his friends, "Artemus Warlock," continued the Professor Blot tradition of adventure tourism. At the time of their trip, in 1891, Arthur was 16, but already his talent as a novelist was evident, and his account of his tour down the Thames — "The Confabulatory Canoeist," was published, with cartoon-like illustrations, in *Chips*, his school's literary magazine.[59] (See fig. 7.) The account, although short, seems to have been inspired by Professor's Blot's tale. However, Stringer's tone is more playful and filled with boyish humour: "The Byron dam was safely shot (not with a gun), being low and sloping."[60]

And like Professor Blot, young Stringer concludes his account with advice to other paddlers:

> If you calculate going for one week, take provisions for *four* weeks. Do not attempt to make the journey
> in a rowboat, but in a light canoe, and this must not be burdened down with too much provisions …
> Do not start in the "dog days," or you will be roasted, but choose the spring, when the water is high
> and the river-bed clear … If you have a bitter enemy, persuade him to take a trip down the Thames in
> August, with two days' rations. It is a lingering and torturing death.[61]

Conclusion

From the late eighteenth and through the nineteenth century, the Thames was a destination for many people. In the end, the reasons for travel, be it discovery, adventure or pleasure, were always satisfied. Each traveller saw the river differently, but most recognized its importance as a resource of considerable value. Alarmingly, by the end of this period came an indication that the river and its watershed were showing the effects of excessive use. As young Arthur Stringer observed to would-be tourists: "Do not drink the river water before straining it through a colander."[62]

58. William Lees Judson, *Kühleborn*, p. 132.
59. Arthur J. Stringer, "A Confabulatory Canoe Trip," pp. 25-30. The magazine was a publication of the London Collegiate Institute.
60. Arthur J. Stringer, "A Confabulatory Canoe Trip," p. 26.
61. Arthur J. Stringer, "A Confabulatory Canoe Trip," p. 30.
62. Arthur J. Stringer, "A Confabulatory Canoe Trip," p. 30.

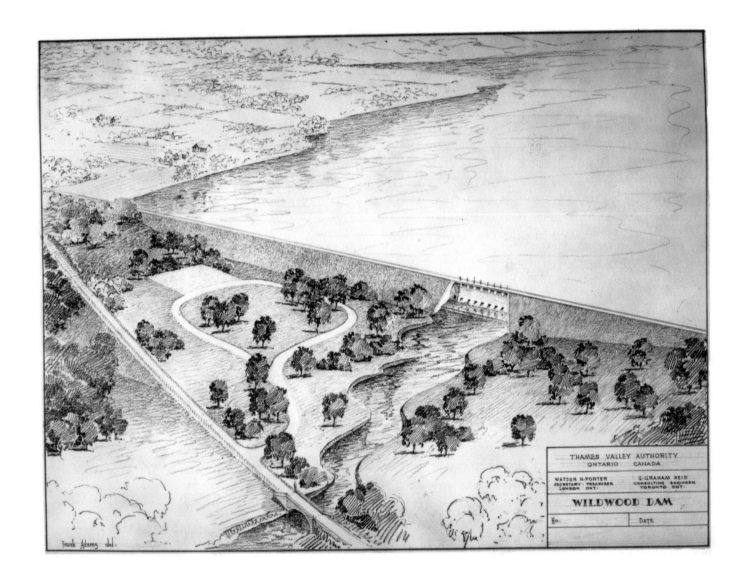

The Constructed Landscape

by George Thomas Kapelos

INTERPRETATIONS OF THE THAMES are powerful and persistent. *Course Studies* takes its cues from a resurgence of interest in landscape, which has occurred in North America and Europe in the second half of the twentieth century. Although *landscape* has existed as a concept for several centuries, in more recent decades there has been a shift in thinking, from landscape as object to landscape as subject, from noun to verb. No longer viewed as a static entity for study, landscape is an agent of cultural activity and action. This shift is mirrored in the activities and actions of the many groups and individuals whose work contributed to the designation of the Thames as a Heritage River, part of Canada's Heritage River System, in 1999. The background document to this nomination presented a clear case for designation, reflecting a broad range of criteria and categories, some easily quantifiable, others less tangible, but all accessible and comprehensible.[1] While each of the categories under which the river was examined in itself does not constitute absolute terms for the river's designation, the whole is clearly greater than the sum of its parts.

Fig. 8. Wildwood Dam, Bird's Eye View c.1950. Frank Adams, delineator, for the Thames Valley Authority.

Upper Thames River Conservation Authority

An artist's rendering of Wildwood Dam on the North Branch of the Thames River depicts the proposed reconstruction of the river and its surrounding landscape.

1. Thames River Background Study Research Team, *The Thames River Watershed*.

What interests me most about the nomination document and process is the equanimity in which diverse subjects of natural and human history are addressed. These components come together in what I call a *constructed landscape*. (See fig. 8.) For me as an architect and urbanist, the construction of our landscape merits our attention.

The idea of the constructed landscape has currency. In his introduction to *Recovering Landscapes: Essays in Contemporary Landscape Architecture*, James Corner explores the opportunities presented by landscape. He argues that landscape contains the idea of "bigness" both in terms of scale and scope. While a landscape can embrace nature and experiences of nature, it also contains within it understandings of culture, social constituency, politics, program and ecological processes. Landscape can no longer be viewed as an object, or something that can be formally understood or manipulated. Rather, landscape as an activity must be about making and marking *Place*.

Using this paradigm for the process of researching *Course Studies* exposes various qualities of this river that in turn suggest possible ways of thinking about it. For example, *Order, System* and *Time* are useful metaphors or *tropes* for understanding the Thames. These tropes when brought together create *Place* and the experience of *Place*. Although this experience is individual and subjective, this concept of *Place* explains the river's imprint on collective memory for those who have lived in and have come in contact with the watershed. Understanding the centrality of *Place* reconstructs this landscape in a way that binds the environment around us to our identity within it.

Order

For the generation born in London after 1950, flooding is a distant historical event. Before that time, it could safely be said that there was no one living in London who did not have some personal recollection or association with river floods. Since the arrival of European settlers, flooding on the Thames has been a well-documented and persistent problem.[2] Historic accounts are vivid and dramatic, but without our personal experience of them, past events remain abstractions to us. Kenneth D. McTaggart wrote in *London's Darkest Hours*: "unless one has experienced a flood firsthand, there is little appreciation for the devastation that occurs; how water can ruin so much so easily; how life can be swept away within the grasp of a hand, and how one's life can be completely ruined."[3]

2. For a list of recorded floods and freshets on the Thames, 1792 to 1951, see *The Thames River Watershed*, Appendix, Table 23.
3. McTaggart, *London's Darkest Hours*, p. 26.

For Londoners of the pre-Second World War generation, the 1937 flood remains vivid and memorable. Grace Williamson, born in 1904, is typical of those who were affected by this flood. From the window of her home on Rogers Avenue she saw water several inches deep coursing down her street. She escaped in pyjamas and returned several days later to a house in shambles. "The clean up was terrible," she described. "We just took the hose into the house and turned it on … You can still see the dark stain under my end table. We had to put cheaper wallpaper on because the water-stain kept weeping through. Eventually everything dried out."[4] For Grace Williamson, as with many other Londoners, the tangible reminder of the flood remained long after its memory had passed. Flood as *stain* — a persistent reminder — tracks through all understandings of the human relations to the Thames. The subsequent putting-house-in-order was not a singular experience, but became the collective approach to the river.

Images of earlier floods make these more distant events tangible and immediate. Paul Peel's sketches of the flash flood of July 11, 1883, although highly stylized, spread news of the extent of devastation and human suffering to readers of the *Canadian Illustrated News*. (See fig. 9.) Following a spectacular mid-summer electrical storm, the flood caught many people at home, asleep, and 11 people were drowned. The event even inspired James McIntyre, Ingersoll's "Cheese Poet" to write:

> At London where two branches join,
> It seem'd two furies did combine,
> For to spread far both death and woe,
> With their wild raging overflow…
> Flood o'er charged both vale and ridges,
> And swept railroads, dams and bridges.[5]

Sentimental and dramatic by contemporary tastes, McIntyre captured human feelings of the time — helplessness, unavoidable and inevitable. By the mid-twentieth century, however, such attitudes had changed.

Fig. 9. The Flood of 11 July 1883.

London Room, London Public Library

The flood of July 1883 on the flats of West London, drawn by Paul Peel for the *Canadian Illustrated News*.

4. Israels, *Londoners Remember*, 1989, p. 14.
5. Charles S. Buck, "Great London Flood of July 11, 1883, Caused 11 Deaths, Widespread Damage," *London Free Press*, 28 July 1956.

Invented as a distinct discipline in Britain at the beginning of the twentieth century, the science of planning developed into a means for ordering and directing growth. In 1922 Thomas Adams, an important early twentieth-century planning advocate, urged the City of London not to allow "building of any kind on lands subject to flood and [the City to] acquire as many of these lands as possible for additional playgrounds and parkways."[6]

Adams' recommendations were consistent with the times. Prior to 1937, efforts to control flooding in southwestern Ontario had been localized and uncoordinated. Dams and other constructions were seen as causes of river flooding as much as agents of its control. It was understood that what might be done in one locale to control a flood might well exacerbate the situation further downstream. However, the means for developing one plan of action to serve all regional constituencies was not in place, nor was the political will in effect to do so. It was widely promoted that through the development of comprehensive planning localized efforts could be coordinated. Other benefits could also include public health, recreation grounds and improved civic amenities.

In the United States regional planning had taken hold in the 1930s. Advanced through organizations such as the Regional Planning Association of America and the writings of Benton MacKaye,[7] regional planning was seen as the solution not only to resource management, but also as a means of economic development at a much larger scale. In Ontario, resource management had come into practice in the early 1920s, although specific initiatives could be found as early as the late-nineteenth century.[8] The focus reflected constituent interests of farmers, lumbermen, and, to a lesser extent, recreational fishermen. However, early on, links were made between resource exploitation and conservation. In 1931 the Federation of Ontario Naturalists was chartered, with a number of local chapters including Chatham and London. The economic depression of the 1930s resulted in farm abandonment and the deterioration of lands through poor land management practices. Attention was turned to the connection between conservation and management. For example, Watson Porter, managing editor of *The Farmer's Advocate* magazine, was instrumental in encouraging soil conservation and reforestation. The 1937 flood catalyzed thinking about larger-scale, longer-term solutions. Despite the demands of World War II, private and government interests moved toward a plan for resource conservation and management.

A meeting at the Ontario Agricultural College on April 25, 1941, was critical. "The Guelph Conference," as it was

6.   Adams, *Report on Town Planning Survey of the City of London.*
7.   The history and impact of the RPAA is contained in Sussman, *Planning the Fourth Migration.*
8.   For a history of conservation activities in Ontario to 1967, see Lambert, *Renewing Nature's Wealth.*

later called, brought together representatives of a wide variety of constituent groups and produced an unsettling report documenting the impoverishment of Ontario's soil through loss of fertility. [9] Successive tiling of fields had severely affected drainage patterns. Water sources were quickly disappearing; water quality was seriously compromised through activities such as drainage of marshes and swamps, and water that did flow into rivers and lakes was polluted by industrial and human waste; forests were being depleted; erosion was increasing; and the overall impact on humans and wildlife was significant.[10] The importance of these findings could not be underestimated, and conservation in Ontario took on a life of its own. In 1944 the provincial government was urged to establish a conservancy act, based on similar legislation in Ohio. At the same time a survey was undertaken of the Upper Thames River watershed and presented at a public gathering in autumn 1946. The idea of regional control of the watershed became paramount.[11]

In the midst of all this planning, flooding reoccurred, in April 1947. Although less severe in London than in 1937, the flood affected communities downstream with an equal impact. London's Mayor George Wenige responded emphatically: "We must see that a threat like this never comes again."[12] Action was swift. On May 27, 1947, a meeting was called to create one river authority. The idea was defeated by a vote of all municipalities within the watershed. Another vote was held in St. Mary's on August 14, 1947 — this time for only those municipalities in the Upper Thames — and the results led to the creation of the Upper Thames River Conservation Authority (UTRCA), the sixth such authority in Ontario.[13]

Two 1947 newspaper photographs are compelling. (See figs. 10 and 11.) In one image, the anxiety on the face of a woman stirs us; she is clutching something of value and sitting in a boat guided to shore through the April flood by four burly firemen. In a contrasting image, a roomful of men participates in the August vote to establish a conservation authority. They are farmers, for the most part: white shirts and ties frame tanned skins, sunburned necks and work-worn hands. The newspaper caption reads: "These pictures taken at the meeting indicate some of the momentous debate..." This vote once again inscribed order on the landscape.

The 1947 establishment of the UTRCA was significant for the construction of the landscape of southwestern Ontario and recalls operations of civilization and culture dating to the establishment of Ontario's European settlements. Any reading of the landscape of the Thames must not overlook previous ordering of the land by

9. Guelph Conference, *Conservation and Post-War Rehabilitation*, February 1942.
10. Masterson, *Herbert Richardson*, p. 50.
11. Dolan documents the early history of the Upper Thames watershed in *Twenty Five Years of Conservation on the Upper Thames Watershed*.
12. *London Free Press*, 7 April 1947, p. 1.
13. The Lower Thames Valley Conservation Authority was organized in 1961.

Fig. 10. The Flood of April 1947.

The London Free Press

"Swiftly rising waters of the south branch of the Thames River forced the evacuation of four families, totaling 25 persons, from the St. Julien bath-house emergency shelter by fire department boat. In this view, two husky firemen pull a boat-load of flood victims to shore."
London Free Press, 7 April 1947.

Swiftly rising waters of the south branch of the Thames River forced the evacuation of four families, totaling 25 persons, from the St. Julien bath-house emergency shelter | by fire department boat. In this view, two husky firemen pull a boat-load of the flood victims to "shore."

First Nations cultures and eighteenth- and nineteenth-century Europeans. The will to conserve, which arose in the mid-twentieth century, was linked causally to previous cycles of exploitation and dereliction that the conservation authorities were mandated to reverse.

As Lynne DiStefano has observed, the Thames was viewed originally as a vehicle to facilitate settlement. As towns developed along its path, a shift in attitudes occurred. The Thames became an obstacle and hindrance to proper development and growth. Various tools have been used to dominate the landscape. Vestiges of these remain in the form of survey and lot division, town settlement patterns, and mill, dam and bridge constructions.

Fig. 11. The Establishment of the Thames Valley Conservation Authority, 14 August 1947.

London Free Press Collection of Photographic Negatives, D. B. Weldon Library, University of Western Ontario

"In a sweeping vote yesterday at St. Marys, 24 upriver municipalities of the Thames River decided to establish a Thames Valley Conservation Authority which will plan a far-reaching program of reforestation, flood control and soil conservation in the Thames Watershed. There was some question as to whether rural or city communities were better represented on the voting list … and this picture shows the rural members standing."
London Free Press, 15 August 1947.

The survey represents the rupture between landscape-as-perceived-wilderness and landscape-as-occupied-territory and marks the first imposition of colonial order on the landscape and the partitioning of land. Together with the road, the survey created the framework for settlement, enabling the movement of goods and people.[14] Prior to Lieutenant Governor Simcoe's arrival at the Forks on March 2, 1793, river surveying had begun. Patrick McNiff undertook the first survey of the river in the fall and winter of 1790 and 1791. His objectives were explicit — to observe the river, noting adjacent conditions and locations for settlement. In the process, McNiff laid out riverfront lots in a number of townships near the mouth (Dover East, Chatham, Raleigh and Harwich, among others). These surveys place the earliest European settlement along the Thames in the late 1790s.[15]

14. See Van Nostrand, "On the Nature of the Road," p. 4.
15. McGeorge, *Early Settlement and Surveys of Kent,* 1924.

The spread of settlement was aided by the development of transportation corridors, new technologies and the location of industries within this system. Bridges and mills are archetypal constructions of the river landscape. Other indicators of settlement, including rural schools, churches and post offices, supported this landscape, but often existed outside the river corridor.[16] The Thames is criss-crossed by bridges — over 300 at the latest count — and their history is well documented. Prior to the enactment of the Municipal Act in 1849, bridge building had been concentrated in the hands of the district government. The Act gave municipalities the unwelcome responsibility of bridge building. "The governments with the least financial resources and technical expertise had unfortunately been saddled with responsibilities they were not yet equipped to deal with."[17] Bridge building was highly susceptible to political pressure, resulting in the variety of structures seen along the river today.

The bridge is an important artefact in understanding the river. A place where road and river meet, the bridge gives travellers a chance to see the river and is often the only place along the river providing access and refuge.[18] While most of the nineteenth-century bridges were of wood, two notable iron bridges of that period are the Fifth Street Bridge in Chatham (See fig. 12.) and Blackfriar's Bridge in London built in 1875 by the Canton Wrought Iron Bridge Company. Still extant, Blackfriar's "ranks among Canada's most significant examples of surviving nineteenth century engineering."[19]

While bridges continue to be essential elements of the Thames landscape, the mill has moved from an integral component on the scene to a picturesque relic. The mill lost its connection to the river as water-driven mills were replaced first by steam and then by electricity. Some mills remain, even continuing to store and house grain, but these are rare. More typical is the story of Hall's Mills, Byron, near the present-day Byron Branch Public Library, commemorated by a plaque. Three successive mills existed on this site, including a water-powered wool-carding machine, cloth factory and tannery. The mill complex also contained a distillery, producing 12,000 gallons of whiskey annually, and a water-powered gristmill, with one run of stone used for grinding grain for the distillery. This mill was destroyed in the summer flood of 1883 and rebuilt, only to be destroyed by fire in 1907. Rebuilt again, it continued operation into the 1920s. According to historian Daniel Brock, "while it is said that this last mill was washed away in the great flood of April 1937, the *London Free Press* made no mention of a flour mill there at the time, but did report that 'a portion of the historic old Byron sawmill, which had withstood the flood of 1883, was carried away by the high water.' With the removal of Byron's third flourmill, an industry of more than 100

16. An extensive inventory of the cultural heritage in the Thames River valley is currently underway under the direction of Michael Troughton, Department of Geography, University of Western Ontario.
17. Cuming, *Discovering Heritage Bridges on Ontario's Roads*, p. 37.
18. Among many references, bridges are discussed in *Thames Topics*, Booklet 6, and in Hamil's *The Valley of the Lower Thames*.
19. Fred Armstrong, *The Forest City*, p. 106.

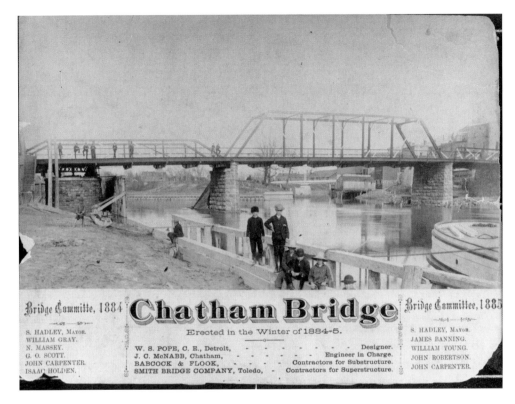

Fig. 12. Fifth Street Bridge, Chatham, 1884.

Chatham-Kent Museum

The first bridge to cross the river at Fifth Street, Chatham, was erected in 1849. Destroyed by fire in 1854, it was rebuilt, only to be carried away by ice in 1868. In 1884, Babcock and Flook and the Smith Bridge Company of Toledo, Ohio built the iron bridge, illustrated here. It continued in use until 1930 when it was replaced by the current bridge.

years' duration passed from the scene. The mill was never rebuilt."[20] The miller's house remains today, still in use as a residence.

Changes to the landscape are a direct result of human actions and large-scale development. From the handful of settlers found along the Thames at the time of Lieutenant Governor Simcoe's visit in 1793, the population of Ontario has grown exponentially: 158,000 in 1825; just under 2 million in 1851; over 4.5 million in 1951; and an estimated 12 million in 2001.[21] Growth in southwestern Ontario is keeping pace with the rest of the province. Along with rapid urbanization and rural restructuring, population growth has had a dramatic impact on the

20. Brock, *A Miscellany of London.*
21. *Historical Atlas of Canada,* University of Toronto, 1997 and *Ontario Statistics,* Ontario Ministry of Treasury and Economics, 1986.

landscape. Today over half a million people live within the watershed, in an area of some 5,825 square kilometers, located in 57 municipal units. Four First Nations are found along the Thames. Of the watershed's population, roughly 75 percent live in urban areas, while the remainder is settled in the cultivated agricultural hinterland. As the nineteenth-century landscape continues to be reconstructed, traces of previous order continue to reappear as palimpsests of the past.

System

Fanshawe Dam, the first major public work of the UTRCA, opened in September 1953 with much celebration.[22] (See fig. 13.) Speaking at the opening, UTRCA Chairman Dr. J. Cameron Wilson announced: "This dam is in no way a challenge to the forces of nature. Beginning here it is our determined purpose to work with nature back and up to the utmost limits of the watershed, endeavouring wherever possible to restore those conditions of soil and forest and swamp and stream and spring as nature created them and, if undisturbed by man, would maintain them forever."[23] The same enthusiasm was echoed ten years later in the groundbreaking for the start of the Wildwood Dam, near St. Marys, when Kelso Roberts, Ontario's Minister of Lands and Forests, called Wildwood a "milestone," and cited the conservation authority as an outstanding example of long-range planning and development. (See fig. 14.) Gordon Pittock, Chairman of the Conservation Authority, boasted that by 1971, when the program was completed, the UTRCA "will be a model for all northeastern North America."[24] Such comments are typical of the hyperbole that underlay the creation of a system of management and conservation for the watershed.

The idea of systems and the underlying concept of ecology can be traced to the writings of George Perkins Marsh, who first introduced the notion of ecological order in 1864.[25] Marsh brought an awareness of interdependencies between humans and the natural world. Systems thinking was expanded and applied to the wider discipline of planning, and conservation was taken up by Aldo Leopold and others.[26]

The underpinning for the conservation authority was an extensive survey undertaken in the summer of 1946. Reports at the time note the enterprise as unusual for its comprehensiveness, use of up-to-the-minute knowledge of soils and land use, and the employment of aerial photography to effect the work.[27] Directing the survey was A. Herbert Richardson, the province's chief conservation officer and a Harvard-trained forester well steeped in

22. The channelization of the Thames at Ingersoll had been completed in 1950 at a cost of $100,000. Fanshawe Dam, costing $4.9 million, was symbolic of the UTRCA's future.
23. *Farmers' Advocate*, 24 October 1953.
24. *London Free Press*, "Spade Ceremony Marks Wildwood Dam Start," 5 June 1963.
25. Marsh, *Man and Nature*.
26. See Leopold's "Land Ethic," in *A Sand County Almanac*.
27. "The Unique Survey on the Thames Watershed," *Farmer's Advocate*, 26 July 1945, p. 527.

Fig. 13. Fanshawe Dam under construction in the winter of 1951–1952.

Upper Thames River Conservation Authority

Built at a cost of $4.9 million across the valley of the North Branch of the Thames above London, Fanshawe Dam is the largest flood control structure in Ontario.

Fig. 14. Groundbreaking, Wildwood Dam, 4 June 1963.

London Free Press Collection of Photographic Negatives, D. B. Weldon Library, University of Western Ontario

Representing the three levels of government were, left to right, John Turner, parliamentary secretary to Arthur Laing, federal Minister of Northern Affairs and National Resources, Gordon Pittock, Chairman of the Upper Thames River Conservation Authority and Kelso Roberts, Ontario Minister of Lands and Forests.

systems approaches to resource management.[28] He also wrote the preliminary report in 1946 and the comprehensive plan of 1952, a weighty 700-page document that continues to inspire awe amongst conservationists.

28. Masterson, *Herbert Richardson*, 1992.

The report was exhaustive in scope and recommendations for land use, water, forestry, wildlife and recreation. In addition, a comprehensive survey of the historical resources of the watershed, undertaken by historian Verschoyle Blake, remains a model study of the social, political and cultural dimensions of a landscape's history. To control flooding, the report recommended the purchase of 30,000 acres of farmland, the construction of six dams (Fanshawe, Glengowan, Wildwood, Woodstock, Cedar Creek, and Thamesford), and a variety of channel improvements. The conservation authority mandated reforestation, pollution control, the reclamation of agricultural land and wildlife preservation. Through the creation of recreation areas in the newly formed parks adjacent to the dam sites, conservation was linked to recreation. Issues were considered exhaustively, the first time in over a century that anyone had viewed the Thames as a complex whole.

The last time the Thames-as-system had any officially recognized importance was in the mid-nineteenth century, when hopes were strong that the river would become a regional waterway. Fred Coyne Hamil's *The Valley of the Lower Thames* ends its narrative at 1850, "when the first railroad was completed and the Thames began to lose its importance as the main unifying influence of the region."[29] River-as-transportation-system was the theme of early narratives and adventures. Records of river commerce at the beginning of the 1800s are plentiful.[30] By 1833 the village of Chatham with a population of only some 25 families was already noted as a centre for building ships and steamboats, an industry started in the late eighteenth-century when the British navy built ships there. As a transfer point between stagecoach to boat for travellers from Niagara to Detroit, Chatham was dubbed the "emporium of the west," with travellers between the eastern and western parts of the United States of America choosing the shorter, Canadian route to the west, rather than the longer route via Lake Erie or land south of the lake.[31] The Chatham *Journal* reported on May 7, 1842 that "A number of schooners are now lying at our wharves and along the banks of the river taking in staves for the Montreal market. It is a cheerful sight to see the tranquil waters of our placid stream studded with masts."[32] However, the arrival of the railway ended ambitions that the Thames could rival other inland waterways as a commercial route.

For the remainder of the nineteenth century and into the 1920s, the river remained a place for passenger excursions. In London, the May 1881 sinking of the steamer *Victoria* near Springbank Park and the horrific loss of lives did not put an end to river outings. Local excursions continued to be a source of diversion, until the street railway became the more fashionable mode. From Chatham, excursion boats continued to operate between docks in the city and Detroit until well into the 1920s. (See fig. 15.) Silting problems within the channel were a

29. Hamil, *The Valley of the Lower Thames*, p. ii.
30. "When People Travelled by Steamboat and Stage Coach," *Chatham Old Boys Reunion Souvenir Album*, 1924.
31. Hamil, *The Valley of the Lower Thames*, p. 262.
32. Hamil, *The Valley of the Lower Thames*, p. 267.

Fig. 15. Thames River, Chatham, c. 1895 – 1905.

F. H. Brown Historical Collection, Chatham-Kent Museum

The steamer, *City of Chatham*, sits at the Rankin Dock, adjacent to the J. B. Stringer Mill, located riverside on King Street, Chatham.

constant impediment. Efforts were made to keep the river navigable by means of channel dredging and the construction of retaining walls and wharves, but these measures were counterproductive. With more dredging the river flowed faster, with subsequent erosion and silting. By the late 1920s, large-scale river traffic had disappeared and expectations that the Thames would provide more than localized transportation had vanished.

The establishment of UTRCA and its report confirms the importance of the river as a system of interdependent resources. Water, soil, land, plant materials and wildlife remain essential components of the system. First, the Thames is a waterway, part of the Great Lakes Basin, and the scope of the waterway has been the subject of interest and control since the river's discovery by Europeans. The 1958 story of the escape of Slippery the Sea Lion

Fig. 16. Cover, *The Day Slippery Ran Away*, by Earle Beattie, illustrated by Merle Tingley.

D. B. Weldon Library, University of Western Ontario

"Slippery lived in a fairy-tale place called Storybook Gardens, and like many storybook people, he decided to run away. He swam off from his little home … and headed for the sea where he had been born. He swam and swam for ten long days … When Phil Skelton of the Toledo Zoo captured him at nearby Sandusky on June 27, 1958, Slippery had swum four hundred miles." Beattie, *The Day Slippery Ran Away*, p. 1.

from Springbank Park's *Storybook Gardens*, which captured the attention of Londoners, is perhaps symbolic. (See fig. 16.) Reports of Slippery-sightings along the river, through Detroit and into Lake Erie, and his recapture some ten days later near Sandusky Ohio, reminded Londoners of their river's connectedness to a larger whole. On his return, Slippery was reunited with his mate, dubbed "Lonesome" as a result of Slippery's escape. "They spent a quiet night together," reported Ted Foster, a Public Utilities Commission consultant. "They obviously had a lot to tell each other."[33] One wonders whether their late night tête-à-tête included Slippery's description of the polluted muck encountered along the way.

Humans impose conflicting demands on the river. Excess flows in the form of floods are to be avoided. Low flows create difficulties for irrigation, sewage disposal and recreation.   Consumption, industry, disposal and irrigation have all been factors. The pump house at Springbank Park (Tracy, Robinson and Moore, 1877) and the adjacent reservoir are relics of nineteenth-century technology, when nearby springs were tapped for the city's use.[34] Vestiges of similar structures can be seen in St. Marys and elsewhere.

Pollution has been a constant issue for the river. "In 1866 an Ekfrid Township man detected a bitter taste to his tea, and he knew why," reported the *London Free Press*. "Londoners, he cried, were emptying their privies into the Thames River."[35] The issues were not much different in 1952 when the UTRCA Report stated "The City of London is potentially the most serious source of pollution on the watershed … Both branches of the river are heavily polluted at London, and the river below London is also foul."[36] Efforts to clean up the river have continued for the

33. *London Free Press*, 8 July 1958.
34. London has been drawing its water from Lake Huron since the mid-1960s.
35. Warren McDougall, "New Lease on Life," *London Free Press*, 16 December 1967
36. UTRCA Report, 1952, Part 3, p. 55.

Fig. 17. Thames River Clean Up, 1970.

London Free Press Collection of Photographic Negatives, D. B. Weldon Library, University of Western Ontario

Gail Major and Stan Smith look over a typewriter found at Fanshawe Dam after an inspection and clean out of the stilling basin in November 1970 while an unidentified woman looks on.

37. Author's notes to presentation "Thames Water Quality Report Card," presented by Ingrid Taylor, Water Quality Specialist UTRCA, *Thames River Symposium*, London, April 7, 2001.
38. Sandra Postel, in a speech to the Annual Meeting of the Canadian Institute of Planners, Charlottetown PEI, July 2000.
39. Discussion with Cathy Quinlan, UTRCA, June 2001.
40. Perhaps one of the most succinct descriptions of the Thames as an ecosystem can be found in a commentary by Steve Hicock, "Progress threatens Thames Valley," *London Free Press*, 3 March 1990.

past thirty years. (See fig. 17.) Although regulations have changed, 50 years later the issue remains. Ingrid Taylor, water quality specialist with the UTRCA, recently presented the 2001 *Thames Water Quality Report Card* as part of the UTRCA *Watershed Reports*. Her research revealed that the best water quality was evident near Komoka Creek, Gregory Creek, and in the North Thames near Plover Mills. The worst was at Dingman Creek. Spills continue to be a source of degradation, with 113 reported in the London area since 1988.[37]

Water and water quality are universal issues. Sandra Postel, Director of the Global Water Policy Project, predicts that global limits to access and use of water may be closer than we think. Worldwide, she advises, we are already using about half the accessible, readily available surface water runoff. The damming of rivers has created serious ecological consequences. Many major rivers are tapped out at peak demand, including dry seasons of the year. Tapping of groundwater and large-scale irrigation has exacerbated river flows. Postel projects a gap between demand and supply, and estimates that we will need the equivalent of ten more Nile Rivers over the next 30 to 40 years.[38] For the Thames, *Watershed Reports* will continue to assess water quality and monitor it in relation to the Great Lakes Basin.

Since 1950, the conservation authority has shifted from being a large-scale intervener to a more agile player with an adept touch. The shift to ecological planning and "soft engineering" has been gradual, but deliberate.[39] Emphasis has been on the use of regulations to deter incursions into the watershed and to encourage bioengineering techniques. Today, means of conservation less abrupt than dams, channels or gabion baskets are utilized. This shifting emphasis on ecology has brought attention to the watershed-as-biosphere. As an intricate ecosystem, the Thames is teeming with life.[40] Robert Bailey, a freshwater Ecologist in the Zoology Department of the University of Western Ontario, poetically described one moment in this system:

> Imagine for a moment that we are wading the river just downstream of Fanshawe Dam in late August. There is a thick carpet of filamentous algae on the rocks, and if we look carefully among the strands of algae, we see many different small insects, crustaceans and molluscs. A few kilometres away, just upstream of there the Medway Creek flows under the Ninth Concession north of Arva, there is relatively little algal growth on the rocks. There, cattails form clumps on little islands in the stream.

Large clams, as big as the palm of your hand, poke out of the bottom to filter small particles of food out of the water. Trees overhang and shade the stream.[41]

Bailey explains the difference in terms of the microbial, plant and animal species in each locale, or what is known as the *community structure*. His specific area of specialization, aquatic ecology, addresses one of many overlapping systems that co-exist and are interdependent within the watershed. The extensive ecology of the region has been documented within the reports nominating the Thames as a heritage waterway.[42] As the only major river in Canada with over 90 percent of its watershed lying within the biologically rich Carolinian life zone, the Thames encapsulates a bioregion found nowhere else in Canada.[43] Coinciding with one of the richest agricultural zones in the country, as well as one of the regions experiencing persistent pressure for urban development, the bioregion continues to be under siege.

Wetland depletion continues to be a source of concern for ecologists. Swamps and wetlands at Ellice, Zorra, Skunk's Misery and Dorchester, to mention the most significant ones, function as sponges, holding water for a slow runoff. About two-thirds of Ontario's 150 native fish species spend some time each year in the Thames, comprising one of Canada's most varied fish communities.[44] The Eastern Spiny Softshell Turtle, often seen sunning itself in the rocky area just below Fanshawe Dam, is one of Canada's rarest turtles and in 1989 was added to Canada's Endangered Species List in the *threatened* category. The watershed is also home to nearly half of the 75 native mammals in Ontario, of which the Southern Flying Squirrel is vulnerable. The Wood Poppy is now so endangered that conservationists are reluctant to disclose its location for fear that such knowledge will lead to its total disappearance.[45]

A corollary to the development of an ecological awareness is the development of recreation along the river, through trails and park systems. In most urban areas, parks and trails have been developed along the river: Mitchell's Centennial Park, St. Marys' Riverview Walkway Park, Stratford's Queen's Park, Woodstock's Fairmont Park, London's Springbank Park and Chatham's Tecumseh Park are all variations of the nineteenth-century pleasure ground established along the river for urban escape and recreation. As the urban areas have expanded, so have these systems, but most remain confined within the boundaries of their communities. One exception is the Avon and Thames Valley Trail, extending along the river through St. Marys along the North Thames, through

41. Robert Bailey, "Aquatic Ecology," in Caveney, 1996.
42. See "Part 1 – Natural Heritage," in *The Thames River Watershed*, pp. 14 –50.
43. "Changing Environment," *Thames Topics*, Booklet 3, Urban League of London, 1999.
44. "Changing Environment," *Thames Topics*, Booklet 3, Urban League of London, 1999.
45. An exhaustive examination of wildlife resources of the watershed can be found in *The Thames River Watershed*. A detailed description of the natural heritage of the river is included in Caveney.

London, to Dingman Creek and south to Delaware. The trail is perhaps the most extensive public connection to the river that can be found along its length. Started in 1968, one-third of the trail travels along private lands. Its existence is due to "public spirited landowners [who] give permission for people to walk through their property."[46]

Frustrating to river-watchers, explorers and students of the river landscape is the limited access found along its length. In some cases the Thames is invisible and episodic, only accessible through travel by canoe or other water means, or from the more privileged view of the aerial adventurer. The trail promises access to the entire river system.

Time

In July 1965, Don Guard, London's planning director, along with former alderman Peter Betts and his wife canoed from Fanshawe Dam to Gibbons Park in London. "The canoe wound and threaded its way as the river meandered through bucolic and sylvan scenes, past sequestered riparian retreats, until its occupants felt almost hushed by the solitude."[47] Noting the suspension of time and place in the experience of the river, Guard observed, "except for the bridges and perhaps a dozen buildings that you can see from the river, you'd have no idea you are passing through a city. It's just like out in the wilds." For the reporter, "from the vantage point of a canoe … London looks much the way it must have appeared to Peter MacGregor when he built his log cabin at the forks of the Thames in 1826."

These sentiments are typical of the constructions of time inspired by the Thames and perpetuated through Western cultural experiences of this landscape. The river flowing through time and carrying memories remains a powerful emblem. Not surprisingly, much of the Thames is about its history and past. This may explain why the waterway's original names — *Akunessippi (Antler River)*, given to it by the Attawandaron, and *La Tranche (The Trench),* named by the French — have been erased. In 1792 Lieutenant Governor John Graves Simcoe rechristened the river as *Thames.* This name, with loftier ambitions and imperial associations, replaced earlier names describing the river's form and landscape.

Marking time continues to preoccupy the construction of this landscape. (See fig. 18.) Four events are significant

46. Thames Valley Trail Association, *A Guide to Hiking the Thames Valley Trail,* p. 1.
47. Joe McClelland, "Little Seen for River Little Changed from Century Ago," *London Free Press,* 4 July 1965.

Fig. 18. Fanshawe Pioneer Village, 1982.

London Free Press Collection of Photographic Negatives, D. B. Weldon Library, University of Western Ontario

"An old-fashioned horse-drawn wagon ride was one of the ways the Upper Thames River Conservation Authority treated guests attending its 35th anniversary celebration. The team of Percherons, Ace and King, was driven by Howard Thornton." *London Free Press*, 16 July 1982, Ed Heal, Photographer.

moments in the river's history: the two battles of the War of 1812 (Moraviantown, 1813, and Longwoods, 1814), the Victoria Boat Disaster, May 24, 1881, the floods of April 1937 and 1947 (and the subsequent creation of conservation authorities), and the declaration of the Thames as a heritage waterway in 1999. Each event contains within it a beginning and an end, or turning points in views to the river: battles that end wars and usher in settlement, a disaster that ends a period of innocence and river travel, another disaster that calls for order and control, and finally a symbolic signaling of a new beginning. Plaques and monuments mark these events and places.

Attempts to represent history abound. (See fig. 19.) The museum at Fairfield Village overlooking the Thames contains artifacts of the Moravians, who arrived with the Delaware First Nation and were the first European

Fig. 19. The Battle of the Thames, Reenactment, Chatham, July 1, 1967.

G. James Photographic Collection, Chatham–Kent Museum

The "Pageant of the Thames" was part of Chatham's celebrations of Canada's Centennial.

settlers on the Thames. Other museums venerate significant episodes in the river's history: the Underground Railroad in Buxton, the genteel life of the colonial elite at London's Eldon House, and early industry at Ingersoll's cheese museum. For river historian Ken McTaggart, the Thames has been a place to dive and retrieve nautical history: "When other people look [at Springbank Park] they see grass and water; but I see steamers and riverboats and all that history."[48]

Contemporary underpinnings of history are found in the new constructions of modernism — recreation and leisure time. Renewed interest in past time is linked to the creation of leisure time, which according to cultural critic Alex Wilson "creates the space, where we look for meaning in our lives."[49] This meaning, Wilson asserts, is

48. "Riverboat's Remains Discovered," *London Free Press,* 20 May 1978, p. 1.
49. Wilson, *The Culture of Nature,* p. 20.

found through tourism and outdoor recreation, which have led to a "massive conceptual reorganization of the landscape."[50] Such is the case with the Wildwood, Fanshawe and Pittock conservation areas, prototypes for the new nature aesthetic, where a large portion of the landscape has been devoted to the creation of recreational areas under the rubric of conservation. (See fig. 20.) In these areas, a different relation to nature has been created, outside the conventional experiences of urban parks and playgrounds. Where urban parks played a role in providing immediate refuge, conservation areas elevated that experience to the observation and preservation of nature in an entertaining manner.

Wilson also points to the necessity of tourism, recreation and nature as a means of self-reconciliation. "By circulating through the material world," he asserts, "we juxtapose the many contradictions of our everyday lives and try to make them whole."[51] Thus we begin to make sense of the competing and conflicting claims made on the Thames waterway by sport fishermen, canoeists, bird watchers and winter snowmobilers.[52]

Absent from much of the published discussion on time and place are the voices of the First Nations. The awe felt by Don Guard and his fellow river travelers in their 1965 glimpses of the wilderness and untamed nature are consistent with Western thought. Colonial and Enlightenment sentiments continue to separate nature from human work, and support ideas of the protection and preservation of nature. In contrast, Aboriginals have never shared these views. "For them, the natural world is not a refuge — the 'other' to an urban industrial civilization — but a place that is sacred in and of itself. In Native cosmologies, human cultures are compatible with natural systems, and it is a human responsibility to keep things that way."[53] Speaking at a Border Crossing Ceremony in 1952, Chief Jasper Hill explained:

> When our forefathers ruled supreme … they were indeed a happy and carefree people. To them the world and the universe were a giant library and their books were the stones, rocks, brooks, rivers, lakes, trees, flowers, herbs, sun, moon, stars. … The fishes of the laughing waters, the animals in the living forests, the birds of the air taught them how to be brave, courageous and true.[54]

The four First Nations found along the Thames below London are only "the latest stage in a very long

Fig. 20. Water-skiing at Wildwood Conservation Area c. 1967.

Upper Thames River Conservation Authority

Wildwood is typical of the new nature aesthetic, where a large portion of the landscape has been devoted to the creation of recreation areas under the rubric of conservation.

50. Wilson, *The Culture of Nature*, p. 43
51. Wilson, *The Culture of Nature*, p. 21
52. On Fanshawe Lake, for example, sail- and paddle-boating is permitted, but no motorboats are allowed. In Westminster Ponds, conflicts have arisen between those wishing to limit access for fear of damaging the existing ecology and those who view this area as a park, with open access.
53. Wilson, *The Culture of Nature*, p. 25
54. Chief Jasper Hill, "We were here long before anyone else," in *My People: The Delaware Indians*, Karen Logan, editor, n.d.

history of human cultural heritage."[55] Evidence points to settlement dating back some 11,000 years to Paleo-Indian cultures. These and subsequent Archaic, Initial and Terminal Woodland cultures have been well documented through excavations and artefacts, and are represented at the London Museum of Archaeology. Plentiful evidence exists of a rich river-based culture, which regarded the Thames as a major source of fish and other foods. The river also provided an important transition to an agricultural way of life.

Place

Unique to London is the Forks, the place where the two branches of the Thames meet. To Londoners, the river is in large part equated with the Forks. Synonymous with its history, the Forks is an important definer of place. "For visual artists, especially the London Regionalists — Greg Curnoe, Bernice Vincent, Jack Chambers — the river sight/site, its environs and its Forks has generated so many different pictur[es], sometimes, of its heartfelt significance and, sometimes, of ordinary details of its daily existence."[56] The continuing power of the Forks is overwhelming. From constructions of courthouse and jail in the early nineteenth century to later twentieth-century developments, the Forks remains the locus for grand plans by city builders and image-makers. (See fig. 21.) Here, river, history and image converge to define *Place*.

Politics, commerce and engineering impose certain kinds of order on a landscape. Science schematizes its elements, and agents of time may alter its physical appearance. In the end, culture and memory define it. As the river landscape continues to be constructed, our understanding of the Thames remains personal, relating to experience and feeling. "The close, never ceasing relationship with the environment is typical of every inhabited landscape," J. B. Jackson explains. "The political landscape is indifferent to the topography and culture of the territories it takes over, but the inhabited landscape sees itself as the centre of the world, an oasis of order in the surrounding chaos, inhabited by the People."[57]

The inhabited landscape, therefore, becomes the locus of a number of different narratives that create their own definitions of the Thames. Each story has its own perspective, and each storyteller attempts to make sense of his or her own world. The landscape constructed of *Order*, *System* or *Time* contrasts with the landscape of *Place*, created through human experience and imagination, which becomes central to understanding the Thames. A few narratives are illustrative.

55. See *The Thames River Watershed*, Chapter 16.
56. Janice Andreae, cultural critic, personal communication, 4 August 2001.
57. Jackson, *Discovering the Vernacular Landscape*, p. 54.

Fig. 21. Redevelopment of the Forks, London, 1964.

London Free Press Collection of Photographic Negatives, D. B. Weldon Library, University of Western Ontario

"Redevelopment of the forks of the Thames River, approved by London's city council last night, would see a new courthouse indicated by Planning Director Donald Guard's pencil." *London Free Press*, 3 March 1964.

Londoner Reg Fowler, born in 1895, skated along the river in the early 1900s:

When the dams were up at Saunby's Mill, below Blackfriar's Bridge, that created enough water so that you could skate all the way down the river, past the university and up to Adelaide Street. On a moonlight night, you could see the people skating down below the Oxford Bridge. It was definitely colder then.[58]

58. Israel, *Londoners Remember*, p. 63.

Historian Orlo Miller, born in 1911, experienced the river's wildness as a boy:

> In the summer that area of Gibbon's Park was a wilderness in the best sense of the word. The river itself was our swimming hole … The north branch was also good for fishing. The last time I went fishing I caught a beautiful five-pound bass.[59]

Jim and Lisa Gilbert retold the tale of Orval Shaw, "the Elusive Hermit of Skunk's Misery," a popular Kent County character of the 1920s and 1930s:

> Orval Shaw resurfaced on the local crime scene in 1928. … Hunted as the prime suspect in a spate of robberies … he persistently avoided capture by hiding out in Skunk's Misery, a dismal wooded area of swamps and dense underbrush near Bothwell. Shaw knew the area like the back of his hand, and it took … many attempts and a posse of fifty men to finally trap Shaw. … In their desperation to capture "the elusive hermit of Skunk's Misery" … [the police force] was made the laughing stock of Ontario. One enterprising stockbroker even listed "Shaw Preferred" on his list of stocks and was offering 10-1 odds that Shaw would elude the police.[60]

Captain Paul McPherson, head of the London Fire Department diving team, dragged the river for bodies in the 1970s and 1980s:

> The river is very deceiving … at the foot of Springbank Dam swirling currents produce a "drowning machine" … It's enough to make your hair stand on end. I've seen lots of little people pull big people under. One time we found a 14-year-old boy and a nine-year-old boy locked together. I don't keep track of it any more — I've got kids of my own.[61]

Skating, fishing, hiding out or drowning — for each of the narrators the Thames has its own particular meaning. Each place — millpond, swimming hole, swamp or whirlpool — while objectively identifiable, cannot be described definitively. Each spot, linked to memory, has its own interpretation, which has grown from an individual's specific experience of the place. This interpretation creates a distinct voice of the landscape, spoken

59. Israel, *Londoners Remember*, p. 107.
60. Gilbert, "Orvil Shaw, the Elusive Hermit of Skunk's Misery," in *There was a time* …
61. Pat Currie, "Quality of river a debatable affair," *London Free Press*, Monday, 11 August 1986.

to and uniquely heard by each of us. This language of landscape is different from that of the planner, ecologist or historian, who all attempt to establish a means of deciphering and understanding the river.

The transformation of landscape-as-metaphor to landscape-as-place continues to operate through the mind and heart of the beholder. Taken collectively, the *tropes* of *Order*, *System* and *Time* seen through the lens of individual experience, the *vernacular*, define the river as *Place*. *Place* becomes "a set of habits and customs accumulated over the centuries, each the outcome of a slow adaptation to a place — to the local topography and weather and soil, and to the people, the superfamily which lived there."[62]

62. Jackson, *Discovering the Vernacular Landscape*, p. 54.

Picture

by George Thomas Kapelos

The Thames-as-subject has fostered considerable production by visual artists — painters, photographers, and filmmakers — all of whom seek to interpret the river using their chosen medium.[1] For the exhibition *Course Studies,* the camera was deliberately selected as the means to track the river, through the lens of photographer Steven Evans, who shot black and white images using a four-by-five-inch view camera.

While the camera provides a particular means of viewing the river, the photographic image has many variants. Until the camera came into widespread use, narrators of events and places had to rely upon the written word or the artist's rendering to capture a moment. Such means, however, were subject to hyperbole and artistic license, as Lynne DiStefano has documented, and as Paul Peel's imagistic rendering of the 1883 London flood so clearly demonstrated. But it is not the intent here to belittle these artefacts of the river's story. Rather, it is possible through photography and the act of photographing to approach another understanding of the Thames landscape. Just as we construct a reading of a landscape, which is subjective and personal, a photograph provides another layer of meaning. Two photograph-types are discussed here: found photographs of the river experience and Steven Evans' commissioned works.

Fig. 22. The Currey Family, Woodstock, 1909.

Currey Collection, Woodstock Museum

David F. Currey, Elizabeth Currey and their daughter Clara, Woodstock Business College Picnic, 1909. The woman's look of delight brings us into the moment of the shutter's click.

1. See, for example, Barry Fair's *Down by the Riverside;* "Inspired by the Thames," *Thames Topics,* Booklet 7; and Lionel Bebensee's 1980 film "La Tranche C'est Moi /The Thames, That's Me!"

Fig. 23. The Detroit Yacht Club Visit to Chatham, 1908.

F. H. Brown Historical Collection, Chatham–Kent Museum

"A rosy dream for some years, the project of a cruise by the Detroit Motor Boat Club to Chatham became a reality on June 13, 1908 … The riverbanks, the bridges and Tecumseh Park, where the landing stage had been built, were black with people. The cannon on the larger cruisers fired salutes; the band on the bank played 'The Star Spangled Banner' and 'God Save the King' — which the visitors mistook for 'America'." Victor Lauriston, *Romantic Kent*, p. 696, Photograph, N. C. Gibson.

A corollary to the exhibition research has been sifting through existing photographs of the river. These photographs come from many sources and are a reflection of the photograph's many roles. Newspaper photographs capture drama and emotion. Promotion shots exude civic pride. Postcards depict idealized, wish-you-were-here moments. Snapshots freeze intimate moments for public scrutiny. Artistic images create ethereal and picturesque scenes. As much as possible all these types of images have been used as illustrations.

Thus a photograph found amidst the Currey Collection in the Woodstock Museum, typical of countless riparian snapshots, has the potential to carry additional meaning. (See fig. 22.) Dated 1909, a pencil note on the back describes the scene: "The Curreys — W. B. C. Picnic." The collection contains other photos, many undated,

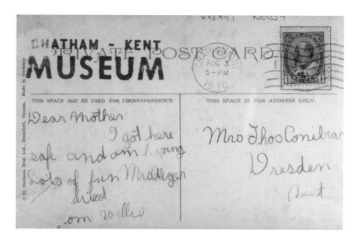

showing the Curreys with their friends and relatives, in a variety of poses, at work, on picnics and enjoying other excursions. Only one other reference to this event emerges, from a photograph that identifies Miss Clara Currey (the little girl in pigtails pictured in the middle of the boat), as a McMaster University graduate of 1926. After graduating, she returned to Woodstock to become a teacher. One wonders what image of the river she carried with her. Was it as strong and equally compelling as those of other storytellers, whose words, not images, continue to exist in time? Has this image moved into our collective consciousness through Miss Currey's recollections to others, or through its mere presence?

"Every photograph is a certificate of presence,"[2] Barthes states, just as every narrative or story records an event. Sometimes the two converge. This is brought home in a pair of images of the visit of the Detroit Yacht Club to Chatham in the summer of 1908. (See fig. 23.) A view of this event captures an unknown photographer at work. Two years later, Willie Conibear sends a postcard — the likely output of this same photographic studio — to his mother in nearby Dresden, Ontario. (See fig. 24.) Reporting on his visit, he writes "Dear Mother, I got here safe and am having lots of fun." Banalities aside, the place and its experience have become one, and this connection makes the photograph so compelling a medium. The photograph "belongs to that class of laminated objects whose two leaves cannot be separated without destroying both: the windowpane and the landscape … desire

Fig. 24. Post Card: *Detroit Motor Boat Fleet at Tecumseh Park, Chatham, Ont., Canada.*

Chatham–Kent Museum

Message to Mrs. Thos Conibear, Dresden, Ontario. Postmarked Chatham, 3 August 1910. 5 p.m. "Dear Mother, I got here safe and am having lots of fun. Mrs Alger [indecipherable]. From Willie."

2. Roland Barthes, *Camera Lucida*, p. 87.

and its object; dualities we can conceive but not perceive."[3] Thus it is impossible to separate the object, the photograph, from what it is portraying, the Thames, as its subject.

A photograph therefore fluctuates between objective record and subjective account. As we enter the landscape by means of the photograph, we recall our own experiences and memories and create our own place. Just as we settle into this reflective state, the photograph flings us out again. We are reminded that we are looking at a representation and, rather than viewing the landscape, we examine the photograph, rendering subject into object, and in this case, museum object. But is this objectification necessarily the end result? Is this an irreversible exercise? What then do we expect of photographs of the Thames? Romantic interpretations of bucolic landscapes and languid waters? Stunning vistas or familiar cosy corners? While there are certainly some images like that, Steven Evans' photographs may come as a surprise, for photographs make visible the unseen.

The assignment to photograph the river, while specific, remained open ended. The objective was not to document the river photographically, but to use photography to explore the Thames. In photographing the river another operation came into play. French philosopher Roland Barthes distinguishes two elements in the photograph that compel our interest. The first is the *studium*, or the general area of interest, and the second is the *punctum*, that particular point that draws us into the photograph and gives us pause. With Roland Barthes as my guide, I have identified "two elements whose co-presence established … [a] particular interest…"[4] First the river exists as a general subject, and then the human element defines the river as territory for human occupation.

With these basic principles enumerated, sites were identified. The sites included places important in understanding the "story" of the river: constructed / natural, urban / rural, and developed / undeveloped. One principle — keeping the river always in the image — both constrained and liberated the process. Certain sites, important in understanding the wider watershed, were visited but not photographed. For example, Skunk's Misery — a significant place to the ecology and mythology of the watershed near Bothwell — is not included in the exhibition photographs.

In many places access to the river is difficult. The private nature of the river in these places is overwhelming. Those locales accessible by road include, within the picture frame, dams, bridges or walkways. In urban places the river

3.   Roland Barthes, *Camera Lucida*, p. 6.
4.   Roland Barthes, *Camera Lucida*, p. 25.

has either been celebrated or ignored. The experience along the river is discontinuous. Few moments of flow, continuum or sequence can be easily enjoyed. Despite these obstacles, an array of images has been produced. Of almost 300 images, 55 are hung in the exhibition and some three dozen are reproduced here. These present sites, some publicly accessible, others usually hidden from view. Layers of history abound, with abandoned bridge abutments reflecting new road alignments, dams or spillways, suggesting the former presence of mills or ponds. In many places human occupation and habitation are evident. An enigmatic circle of stones, a well-placed aluminum lawn chair, a graffiti-covered pier, a carefully-channelled stream complete with stone or cement retaining walls, all tell of human interaction with the river. As Steven Evans returned from his forays into the watershed, each image further revealed the river's complex picture. In doing so, the photographer's images reinforced the curatorial direction of *Course Studies*: the flow between Thames as subject and Thames as object.

The presentation of photographs is sequential and follows the course of the river. First, images are depicted that trace the river's branches upstream and then as it passes through London. Views of the river as it flows westward past the four First Nations, through Chatham and on to Lake St. Clair, conclude the exhibition. The location and date of each image are identified; the contents are not described in detail. Rather, viewers are invited to discover their own impression of the river.

Exhibition Images

by Steven Evans

(detail) St. Marys, Summer 2000

Pittock Dam, Woodstock, Fall 2000

Cement Plant, Beechville, Spring 2001

Beechville, Fall 2000

Ingersoll, Spring 2001

Brooksdale, Spring 2001

Embro, Spring 2001

River View, Thamesford, Fall 2000

Feed Mill, Thamesford, Fall 2000

Mitchell, Spring 2001

St. Marys, Fall 2000

Avon River near Shakespeare, Spring 2001

Avon River near Stratford, Spring 2001

Avon River, Stratford, Spring 2001

Plover's Mill, Winter 2000

Rowing Centre at Fanshawe Lake, London, Summer 2001

Fanshawe Dam, London, Summer 2001

Bridge, University of Western Ontario, London, Summer 2001

London, Spring 2001

Blackfriar's Bridge, London, Summer 2001

The Forks, London, Winter 2001

Pump House, Springbank Park, London, Spring 2001

Springbank Park, London, May 2001

Kilworth, Spring 2001

Delaware, Spring 2001

Delaware, Spring 2001

Delaware, Spring 2001

Big Bend Conservation Area, Summer 2001

Moraviantown – Delaware First Nation, Summer 2001

Thamesville, Fall 2000

Indian/McGregor Creek Flood Control Project, Summer 2001

Chatham, Summer 2001

Near Pain Court, Fall 2000

Prairie Siding, Summer 2001

Bradley, Summer 2001

Lighthouse Point, Fall 2000

Lighthouse Point, Fall 2000

Afterword

by George Thomas Kapelos

I BEGAN THIS PROJECT by asking what a river might be. This was the challenge initially offered by *Course Studies*. Somehow, I believed, I could capture the river and make its essence visible and understood. As I proceeded through the project, however, I was drawn to observe and reconsider the images revealed and the voices uncovered against my existing preconceptions, expectations and imaginations.

> The river flowed both ways. The current moved from north to south, but the wind usually came from the south, rippling the bronze green water in the opposite direction. This apparently impossible contradiction, made apparent and possible, still fascinated Morag even after all the years of river-watching.[1]

As Margaret Laurence recognized in the opening to her novel *The Diviners,* the river in her story appears to flow in two directions. There is an uncertainty about its course and its direction. What appears to be may not be so. Similarly a simple image of the Thames carries a double meaning. An 1890 stereoscopic view, part of Barron's

Fig. 25. Fishing near Blackfriar's Bridge, Stereoscope View, Barron's Artistic Series London, c. 1890.

London Room, London Public Library

Through the device of the stereoscope, we are brought into the river, with the water at our feet we can sense the river's flow, and feel its cool depths and wetness.

1.   Laurence, *The Diviners*, p. 1.

Artistic Series entitled *Fishermen,* offers an idyllic scene of London and its riverside. (See fig. 25.) Accompanied by three boys, a man with a fishing pole sits at the water's edge. Behind them, Blackfriar's Bridge spans the Thames, while high above Firbrae House (c. 1870) overlooks the scene. This is the immediate reading of this picture. But the view presents another perspective. Through the device of the stereoscope, we are brought into the river. With the water at our feet we can sense the river's flow, and feel its cool depths and wetness. We shift from observer to participant, drawn to reflect on this or other rivers, and on other subjects, such as timelessness and the passage of time, nature and the flows of life. The simplicity of the scene is multiplied, becoming a variety of places, times and experiences.

The meanings of the Thames are subjective, relative and ephemeral. Finding one definition for this river remains elusive.

Bibliography

Adams, Thomas. *Report on Town Planning Survey of the City of London*, 1922.

Aikins, Charles. "Journal of a Journey: From Sandwich to York in the Summer of 1806." *Ontario Historical Society: Papers and Records* 6 (1905).

Alexander, James Edward. *L'Acadie, or, seven years' exploration in British America*. Vol. 1. London: Colburn, 1849.

Anonymous. *The Canadian tourist: accompanied by a map of the British American provinces and an appendix containing useful statistical information*. Montreal: Ramsey; Toronto: Armour; Quebec: Sinclair; Three Rivers: Stubbs; Sherbrooke: Brooks; Montreal: Dawson and Miller; Ottawa: Bryson; Kingston: Duff; Port Hope: Ansley; London: C.W. Coombe, 1856.

Armstrong, Frederick H. *The Forest City: An Illustrated History of London Canada*. Windsor Publications, 1986.

Barthes, Roland. *Camera Lucida: Reflections on Photography*. Translated by Richard Howard. Originally published in French as *La Chambre Claire*, 1980. New York: Hill and Wang, 1981.

B[echer], H[enry] C.R. "The Pirate of St. Mary's." *New York Albion,* (7 January 1843), pp.4-5.

Big White Owl (Jasper Hill). *"My People - The Delaware Indians."* Edited by Karen Logan. Copy of unpublished manuscript, Moravian First Nations Library, n.d.

Bonnycastle, Richard Henry. *Canada and the Canadians*. Vol. 2. London: Colburn, 1849.

Bouchette, Joseph. *The British Dominions in North America; or a topographical and statistical description of the provinces of Lower and Upper Canada, New Brunswick, Nova Scotia, the islands of Newfoundland, Prince Edward and Cape Breton. Including considerations on land-granting and emigration. To which are annexed, statistical tables and tables of distances, &c.* Vol. 1. London: Longman, Rees, Orme, Brown, Green and Longman, 1832.

Brock, Daniel J. "Cyrenius Hall and the Byron Grist and Flour Mills." In *A Miscellany of London – Part II*. Compiled by Elizabeth Spicer. *Occasional Paper No. 24*. London: London Public Libraries and Art Museum, 1978.

Caveney, Anita, ed. *Focus on the Thames: Natural and Cultural Heritage of the River*. London: McIlwraith Field Naturalists of London and the Upper Thames River Conservation Authority, November 1996.

Chambers, William. *Things as they are in America*. Philadelphia: Lippincott, Grambo, 1854.

Chapman L. J., and D. F. Putnam. *The Physiography of Southern Ontario*. Toronto: University of Toronto Press for the Ontario Research Foundation, 1951.

Corner, James, ed. *Recovering Landscape: Essays in Contemporary Landscape Architecture*. New York: Princeton Architectural Press, 1999.

Cuming, David J. *Discovering Heritage Bridges on Ontario's Roads*. Erin: Boston Mills Press, n.d.

Curnoe, Greg. *Deeds, Abstracts: The History of a London Lot*. London: Brick Books, 1995.

Curnoe, W. Glen. *Around London 1900 – 1950: A Picture History*. 1973.

Demopoulos, Rai and Mike Baker. *Riverscape to Subdivision*. London: London Regional Art and Historical Museums, 1999.

Disturnell, John. *The Great Lakes or inland seas of North America; embracing a full description of Lakes Superior, Huron, Michigan, Erie, and Ontario; Rivers St. Mary, St. Clair, Detroit, Niagara, and St. Lawrence, Lake Winnipeg, etc., together with the commerce of the lakes: giving a description of cities, towns, etc. forming together a complete guide for the pleasure traveller and emigrant*. New York: Scribner, 1863.

Dolan, T. J. *Twenty Five Years of Conservation on the Upper Thames Watershed 1947–1973*. London: Upper Thames River Conservation Authority, 1973.

Duff, Robert. *London Parks and Recreation 1871–1973: A History of the Recreation Department*. Public Utilities Commission of London, unpublished m.s., June 1973.

Fair, Barry. *Down by the Riverside*. London: London Regional Art and Historical Museums, 1993.

[Fairplay, Francis.] *The Canadas as they now are. Comprehending a view of their climate, rivers, lakes, canals, government, laws, taxes, towns, &c., with a description of the soil . . . derived from the reports of the inspectors made to the justices at Quarter-Sessions, and from other authentic sources, assisted by local knowledge.* Pt. 2. London: Duncan, 1833.

Gilbert, Jim and Lisa. *"There was a time . . ."* In *Historical Anecdotes of Chatham-Kent, Ontario: A Collection.* Edited by Stephanie Groen and Lisa Rumiel. Chatham: Chamberlain Mercury Printing, 1999.

Gourlay, Robert. *Statistical account of Upper Canada, compiled with a view to a grand system of emigration.* Vol.1. London: Simpkin and Marshall, 1822.

Hamil, Fred Coyne. *The Valley of the Lower Thames: 1640 to 1850.* Toronto: University of Toronto Press, 1951.

Howison, John. *Sketches of Upper Canada, domestic, local and characteristic: to which are added practical details for the information of emigrants of every class and some recollections of the United States of America.* 2 ed. Edinburgh: Oliver and Boyd; London: Whittaker, 1822.

Israels, Fred. *Londoners Remember.* London: Ad Ventures in History Inc., 1989.

———. *Londoners Remember, Part Two: A Collection of Reminiscences.* London: Ad Ventures in History Inc., 1993.

Jackson, John Brinkerhoff. *Discovering the Vernacular Landscape.* New Haven: Yale University Press, 1984.

Jameson, Anna Brownell. *Winter Studies and Summer Rambles in Canada.* With an Afterword by Clara Thomas. London: Saunders and Otley, 1838; Toronto: McClelland & Stewart Inc., New Canadian Library, 1990.

Judd, William W. *Diaries of a Trip to Manitoulin Island (1880) and of a Trip down the Thames River (1881) by W. E. Saunders. Edited and with Notes. Occasional Paper No. 26.* London: London Public Library and Art Museum, 1974.

Judson, William Lees. *Kühleborn: A Tour of the Thames.* London: Advertiser Steam Press, 1881.

Lambert, Richard S. with Paul Pross. *Renewing Nature's Wealth: A Centennial History of the Public Management of Lands, Forests and Wildlife in Ontario.* Toronto: Hunter Rose, 1967.

Laurence, Margaret. *The Diviners.* Toronto: McClelland and Stewart, 1974.

Lauriston, Victor, Compiler. *Official Programme of the Old Boys' and Girls' Reunion Held in Chatham, June 29 to July 5, 1924.* Chatham: Old Boys' Reunion Committee, 1924.

———. *Romantic Kent: More Than Three Centuries of History, 1626 – 1952.* Chatham: Corporation of the City of Chatham, 1952.

Leopold, Aldo. "Land Ethic." In *A Sand County Almanac.* London: Oxford University Press, 1987.

Littlehales, Edward Baker. *Journal. With an Introduction by Henry Scadding.* Toronto: The Copp, Clark Company, 1889.

———. "Journal from Niagara to Detroit." In *The Correspondence of Lieutenant Governor John Graves Simcoe.* Edited by E.A. Cruikshank. Vol. 1: 288-293. Toronto: The Ontario Historical Society, 1923.

Lutman, John H. "The London Waterworks." In *A Miscellany of London Part III.* Edited by Elizabeth Spicer. *Occasional Papers No. 26.* London: London Public Libraries, 1980.

Mackay, Charles. *Life and Liberty in America: or, sketches of a tour in the U.S. and Canada in 1857-1858.* New York: Harper, 1859.

Marsh, George Perkins. *Man and Nature.* Edited by David Lowenthal. Boston: Harvard University Press, 1964, originally published 1864.

Masterson, Paul. *Herbert Richardson.* Richmond Hill: Fitzhenry and Whiteside, 1992.

McGeorge, W. G. "Early Settlement and Surveys Along the River Thames in Kent County." *Kent Historical Society Papers and Addresses.* 6 (1924): 5 – 31.

McTaggart, Kenneth D. *The Victoria Day Disaster.* Petrolia: Skinner Printing, 1978.

———. *London's Darkest Hours*. Edited by Debra L. Rogers. London: RBL, 1989.

Meinig, Donald William, ed. *The Interpretations of Ordinary Landscapes: Geographical Essays*. New York: Oxford University Press, 1979.

Morden, Pat. *Putting Down Roots: A history of London's Parks and River*. St. Catharines: Stonehouse Publications, 1988.

Ontario. Department of Planning and Development. *The Thames Valley Report 1946*. Toronto: 1947.

Ontario. Department of Planning and Development. *Conservation in South Central Ontario*. Toronto: 1948.

Ontario. Department of Planning and Development. *Upper Thames Valley Conservation Report 1952*. Toronto: Conservation Branch, 1952.

Ontario. Department of Energy and Resources Management. *Lower Thames Valley Conservation Report 1966 – Summary*. Toronto: Conservation Authorities Branch, 1966.

Ontario. Department of Energy and Resources Management. *Lower Thames Valley Conservation Report*. Toronto: Conservation Authorities Branch, 1966.

Pfaff, Larry. *Historic St. Marys*. St. Marys: J.W. Eedy Publications, n.d.

Pickering, Joseph. *Emigration or no emigration, being the narrative of the author, an English-farmer, from the year 1824-1830 during which time he traversed the United States of America, and the British Province of Canada with a view to settle as an emigrant containing observations in the manners and customs . . . the soil and climate . . .* London: Longman, Rees, Orme, Brown and Green, 1830.

Richardson, John. *Eight Years in Canada: Embracing a review of the administrations of Lords Durham and Sydenham, Sir Chas. Bagot, and Lord Metcalfe; and including numerous interesting letters from Lord Durham, Mr. Chas. Buller, and other well-known public characters, by Major Richardson*. Montreal: Cunningham, 1847.

Saunders, William Edwin. *Diaries of a Trip to Manitoulin Island (1880) and of a Trip Down the Thames River (1881)*. Edited by William W. Judd. *Occasional Paper, No. 16*. London: London Public Library and Art Museum, 1974.

Small, Henry Beaumont. *The Canadian Handbook and Tourist's Guide, giving a description of Canadian lake and river scenery, and places of historical interest with the best spots for fishing and shooting*. Edited by J. Taylor. Montreal: Longmoore, 1866.

Stringer, Arthur J. "A Confabulatory Canoe Trip." *Chips,* March 1891.

Sussman, Carl, ed. *Planning the Fourth Migration: The Neglected Vision of the Regional Planning Association of America*. Cambridge: MIT Press, 1976.

Talbot, Edward Allen. *Five Years' Residence in the Canadas, including a tour through parts of the United States of America in the year 1823*. London: Longman, Hurst, Rees, Orme, Brown and Green, 1824.

Thames River Background Study Research Team. *The Thames River Watershed: A Background Study for Nomination under the Canadian Heritage Rivers System*. London: Upper Thames River Conservation Authority for the Thames River Coordinating Committee, 1998.

Thames Valley Trail Association. *A Guide to Hiking the Thames Valley Trail*. London: 1998.

Urban League of London. *Celebrate the Thames: Educational Pamphlets*. Booklets 1 – 8, 1999.

Van Nostrand, John. *"On the Nature of the Road."* Unpublished Manuscript Delivered to Third Annual Meeting of the Society for the Study of Architecture in Canada, June 1977.

Wilson, Alexander. *The Culture of Nature: North American Landscape from Disney to the Exxon Valdez*. Toronto: Between the Lines, 1991.

Wright, Ian. "Water in the World: Sandra Postel's Conference Keynote Presentation." *Plan Canada*, Canadian Institute of Planners, October, November, December 2000. Vol. 40, No. 5.

Thames Watershed Facts

Names:
Askunesippi, Antler River, La Tranche, The Thames

Area of Drainage Basin:
5,825 square kilometres

Length of Drainage Basin:
200 kilometres

Length along River:
From Lake St. Clair to London is 187 kilometres, from London to Tavistock is 86 kilometres, and from London to Mitchell is 77 kilometres

Highest Elevation:
420 metres east of Stratford

Population:
Approximately 532,000 (1995 data)

Jurisdiction:
All or part of 7 Counties and 57 Municipalities

Fish:
97 of Ontario's 150 fish species

Endangered Species:
37 of 275 in Canada (1996 data)

Water Flows:
In about 36 hours from Tavistock to London and in 3 to 4 days from London to Chatham

Thames Watershed Facts, Urban League of London.
The Thames Our Heritage. Map, 1997.

Map of the Thames Watershed

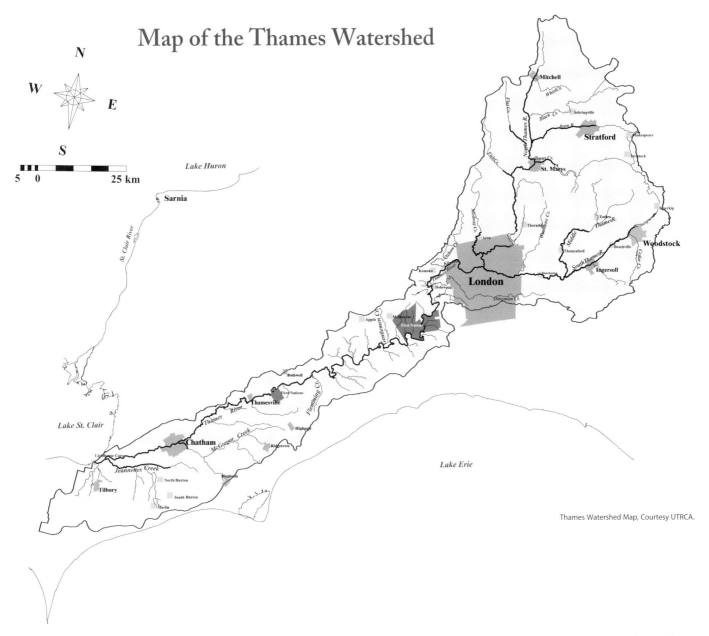

N
W   E
S

5   0   25 km

Lake Huron

Sarnia

St. Clair River

Mitchell

Whirl Cr.

Black Cr.   Sebringville

Avon R.   Stratford   Shakespeare

North Thames R.   Trout Cr.   Tavistock

Fish Cr.   St. Marys

Harrietsville

Medway Cr.   Thorndale   Trout Cr.   Thames R.   Embro

Arva   Thamesford   Middle   Beachville   Woodstock

Cedar Cr.

Komoka   Oxbow Cr.   Dorchester   South Thames R.   Ingersoll

Thames River   London

Delaware

Dingman Cr.

Appin   Muncey First Nation

Gentleman Cr.

Bothwell

Flemming Cr.

First Nations   Thamesville

Highgate

Lake St. Clair

Thames River

McGregor Creek   Ridgetown

Chatham

Lighthouse Creek

Jeannettes Creek   Blenheim

Lake Erie

North Buxton

Tilbury   South Buxton

Merlin

Thames Watershed Map, Courtesy UTRCA.

Acknowledgements

Thanks are given to the following Facilities, Institutions, Organizations and Corporate Entities:

Celebrate the Thames

Chatham-Kent Museum, Tanya Neave, Assistant Curator

Mary Anne Coffey, Editor

First Nations: Chippewa of the Thames First Nation, Joe Miskokomon; Delaware of Moraviantown First Nation, Leighton Hopkins, Darryl Stonefish; Munsee-Delaware First Nation, Mark Peters; Oneida of the Thames First Nation, Harry Doxtator; Government of Ontario Liaison, Dennis Martel

Steven Dale Harding Photography

Harvard University Graduate School of Design, Loeb Library

Kincardine Public Library

London Free Press, Anita McCallum, Librarian

London Public Library, London Room, Arthur McClelland, Librarian

Museum London, Mike Baker, Bob Ballantine, Barry Fair, Brian Meehan, Ruth Anne Murray, Peter Smith

Metropolitan Toronto Reference Library, Baldwin Room, Alan Walker

Ryerson Polytechnic University, Faculty of Engineering and Applied Science, Derek O. Northwood, Dean, Department of Architectural Science and Landscape Architecture, Michael Miller, Chair

The University of Hong Kong, Department of Architecture, Hong Kong, SAR

The University of Toronto, Faculty of Architecture, Landscape, and Design: Pierre Bélanger, Nancy Chater, Gil Delvecchio, Lee Gowan, Andy Payne, Larry Wayne Richards, the late Pamela Manson Smith, Robert Wright, Students in LAN513F and LAN1032H

The University of Western Ontario, D. B. Weldon Library, John Lutman and Theresa Regnier, Benson Special Collections and J. J. Talman Regional Collection

Upper Thames River Conservation Authority, Terry Chapman, Eleanor Heagy, Cathy Quinlan

Woodstock Museum and Cultural Centre, Sheila A. Johnson, Curator, David Schlosser, Collections Assistant

The curator, photographer and contributor wish to make the following personal acknowledgements:

Steven Evans:
Cynthia Blackman, Steve Callahan, Bob Carnie, Dennis Waters, Craig Williams, Ross Winter

Lynne DiStefano:
Doug Bocking, John Bradley, Dan Brock, Glen Curnoe, Joe DiStefano, Matt DiStefano, Andrea DiStefano, Zilpa Howard, Beryl and Dick Ivey, Lee Ho Yin, Paddy O'Brien, Steven Otto, Honor de Pencier, Larry Pfaff, Edward Phelps, Nancy Poole, Chris Power, Betty Spicer, Tom Tausky

George Thomas Kapelos:
Christopher Andreae, Emily Andreae, Janice Andreae, Katherine Ashenburg, Greg Baeker, Elizabeth Baird, George Baird, Megan Bice (and the use of her cottage at Kincardine), Catherine Davin, Sheila Devine, Joe DiStefano, Pamela Fitzgerald, John Fraser, Hugues Goisbault, Hope Hasbrouck, Bessie Kapelos, John Kapelos, Philip Kapelos, James Liabotis, Réjeanne Liabotis, Marybeth McTeague, Steven Otto, Geraldine Sherman, Mary Singeris, Tony Singeris, Merle Tingley, Heidi Williams

Funding for the exhibition and publication has been received from:

The Richard Ivey Foundation
The Government of Canada, Department of Canadian Heritage, Museums Assistance Program
Trojan Technologies Inc.
The Corporation of the City of London

THE RICHARD IVEY
FOUNDATION

Course Studies – Tracking Ontario's Thames: *An Exploration of the River*

George Thomas Kapelos

with

Steven Evans, Photographer

Lynne DiStefano, Contributor

Catalogue to accompany the exhibition, *Course Studies – Tracking Ontario's Thames: An Exploration of the River,* held at Museum London, 10 November 2001 – 13 January 2002.

ISBN 1-895800-61-7

George Thomas Kapelos (born London, Ontario, 1949), Steven Evans (born New York, New York, 1956).

©2001 with Museum London, London, Ontario, Canada on behalf of the authors.

Cover, endpaper: Steven Evans, (detail) St. Marys, Summer 2000

Printed in Canada by Capital Colour Graphics Inc., London, Ontario.

London
CANADA

ONTARIO ARTS COUNCIL
CONSEIL DES ARTS DE L'ONTARIO

The Canada Council | Le Conseil des Arts
for the Arts | du Canada

THE ONTARIO TRILLIUM FOUNDATION
LA FONDATION TRILLIUM DE L'ONTARIO

Museum London gratefully acknowledges the financial assistance of The City of London, The Ontario Arts Council, The Canada Council for the Arts and The Ontario Trillium Foundation

MUSEUM | LONDON

where art and history meet

421 Ridout Street North, London, Ontario, Canada N6A 5H4 519.661.0333 • www.museumlondon.ca